Crazy Quilt

Crazy Quilt
A Patchwork of Yesteryear

Lynn Coffey

Copyright 2019
By Lynn Coffey
All rights reserved, including the right to reproduce this
work in any form whatsoever, without permission in
writing from the author, except for brief passages in
connection with a review.

Cover and interior design by Jane Hagaman
Front cover photo: © Lynn Coffey, vintage family crazy quilt
Back cover photos: © Lynn Coffey (LaRue Fauber Wilson, Lorean Falls Painter,
Mabel Truslow Napier, and Lura Coffey Steele with some of their handstitched quilts)
All current interior photographs by Lynn Coffey
Other family photos in each chapter courtesy of those interviewed
Dedication photo by Jack Jeffers
Russell Lowery chapter photo by Kris Gembara
Early Lyndhurst Train Depot photo courtesy of Augusta County Historical Society
1985 steam locomotive photo courtesy of Danny Hanger
1937 photo of Elk Hill courtesy Virginia Department of Historic Resources
1902 photo of Arthur Ewing courtesy the National Archives
Author photo by Jill Bivens

All the information in the interviews is as told to Lynn Coffey. The
author is not responsible for any misinformation.

If you are unable to order this book from your local bookseller,
you may order directly from the author. Call (540) 949-0329 or
use the order form in the back of the book.

Library of Congress Control Number: 2019905269

ISBN 978-0-578-48986-5
10 9 8 7 6 5 4 3 2 1

Printed on acid-free paper in the United States

Dedicated to all the people who still value the old-time ways and embrace the peaceful, unhurried lifestyle of earlier centuries.

Frank Hatter plowing with his mule, Kate; Love, Virginia
Photo by Jack Jeffers, 1974

ALSO BY LYNN COFFEY

Backroads 1: Plain Folk and Simple Livin'
Backroads 2: The Road to Chicken Holler
Backroads 3: Faces of Appalachia
Appalachian Heart
Mountain Folk

Contents

Foreword, by Kristin Gembara xi
Acknowledgments xv
Introduction xvii
  1. Woodson's Mill, Lowesville 1
  2. Kay Campbell—Floorcloths 23
  3. Robert and June Morris 31
  4. The Lyndhurst Train Depot and Post Office 45
  5. "New Shoes" 61
  6. Jill Bivens—Soap Making 65
  7. Stone Walls 73
  8. The Dodd Cabin, Beech Grove 79
  9. Stephens Grocery 91
10. "Dating Myself by Metal Ice Cube Trays" 97
11. Alice Higgins—Chair Caning 101
12. "Gus" (A Love Story) 111
13. The Jim Snead Cabin, Fork Mountain 121
14. Glenn Wilson—Log Cabin Restoration 133
15. "It's More Than a Wilderness" 147
16. Oak Hill Baptist Church, Massies Mill 151
17. Christmas Traditions in the Blue
    Ridge Mountains 165
18. The Journal: The Childhood Memories of
    Lora Ethel Fitzgerald Allen Matheny 173
19. Elk Hill 185
20. "OCD" 199

21. Homemade Blackberry Juice 203
22. Russell Lowery's Root Cellar 209
23. Beech Grove Christian Church 217
24. Mutt Humphreys—A Day in the Life
    of a Logger 233
25. "Old-Time TV Programs" 245
26. Bob Sales—World War II Veteran 249
27. Apple Schnitzing 259
28. Milford Hartman—A Centenarian Recalls
    One Hundred Years of Living 267

Crazy Quilt

Kristin Gembara

Foreword
by Kristin Gembara

When we were growing up in Chicago, Lynn Coffey's *Backroads* newspaper was a reading staple in our home.

My mother, a Nelson County native, had it delivered to our home for a little taste of country in our inner-city Bridgeport neighborhood. I remember coming home from school and seeing the *Backroads* newspaper lying on the table alongside the daily mail. I devoured it cover to cover while envisioning my mom and her eight siblings living without electricity or running water.

Digesting the *Backroads* newspaper month after month was the kindling that ignited my personal passion for genealogy and sustainable living.

The Blue Ridge Mountains of Nelson County have been home to my mother's people for more than two centuries. The Blue Ridge is the easternmost ridge of the southern Appalachian mountain range. From a distance, the rugged mountains have a gentle blue rolling effect that upon sight eases the soul. Thick with forest, they are filled with an amazing diversity of flora and fauna.

It is one of the oldest mountain ranges in the world, and the old ways of life have never left these ridges. They were old when rivers and streams eroded the rock, forming the waterways we are familiar with today. They were old when the Native Americans lived and hunted there. They were old when immigrant settlers claimed their mountain land patents in the early sixteenth century, giving birth to a mountain way of life.

I am forever grateful for Lynn Coffey's *Backroad* adventures. Through her writings, Lynn has shared with folks from all over a taste of the Blue Ridge and the rich culture of its people. These people I'm honored to call my people.

I've heard Lynn Coffey referred to as the "keeper of the mountain people's stories," and I concur. But she is so much more. This lady doesn't just talk the talk, she walks the walk. She lives her life plain and very simple. An advocate for sustainability before it was mainstream, the *Backroads* publications are chock-full of sustainable lessons and experiences of self-sufficiency from people whose ancestors have occupied the mountains from the beginning of our United States history. These lessons of self-sufficiency are the old mountain people's legacy to this ever-changing world. A legacy that sadly can never be replicated, because of the many modern conveniences we depend on.

Through the remnants of these old mountain ways, we have an opportunity to keep a balance between how we live our lives now and what effects our actions will hold for the next generation. Not just for the Blue Ridge Mountains of Virginia but also for the whole world, including neighborhoods on the southwest side of Chicago.

"I lift up my eyes to the hills, where does my help come from?
My help comes from the Lord, the Maker of heaven and earth."
—Psalm 121:1–2

Note: Kris is a master gardener and genealogist whose family roots lie deep in the red soil of Nelson County, commonly known as "God's Country." She is a close friend and neighbor, writer, confidant, and soul sister when it comes to all things having to do with Appalachian culture and the mountain people in general. I am honored for her to have written the foreword for this sixth book in the Backroads series, *Crazy Quilt*.

Acknowledgments

No one is more amazed than I am that the makings of a sixth book were lying dormant inside me, just waiting for the right time to emerge—first as a thought and later as a constant niggling that this is what I should do. These are the people I'd like to thank for helping me along the long and winding road to writing *Crazy Quilt*.

Gary Allen, who first planted the seed of doing another book in my heart and graciously donated his Grandma Ethel's handwritten journal as one of the chapters.

Kris Gembara, a good friend who honored me by writing the foreword for this new book. She's a faithful compadre who treks up and down the mountains in search of forgotten graveyards, old homeplaces, and other great adventures. She's the one who "gets" me.

My publishing team: Jane Hagaman, Tania Seymour, and Cynthia Mitchell, who have been with me right from the start and together made all six Backroads books look extremely professional in the publishing world.

My grateful heart will always be eternally tender and loving toward Virginia's mountain people who didn't label me as an "outsider" when I moved to the Blue Ridge but tucked me under their protective wings, taught me their ways, and made me one of their own. There are no adequate words to tell you how much you mean to me, only that you've made all my dreams come true, and I love you fiercely!

My loving and very patient husband, Billy, who, twenty-six years ago, not only got a bride but a mountain newspaper and six successive books as well. When I say, "I couldn't have done it without you," it is a literal statement that I mean with all my heart. God could not have blessed me with a more perfect companion, and I am eternally thankful that we found each other.

And speaking of God . . . he is the one who took an ordinary young woman and gave her an unquenchable passion for the old ways. He endowed her with a raw talent for writing and told her to use it in extraordinary ways that would not only fulfill her own heart but also fill the hearts of those to whom she had the honor of talking. Writing their stories has been a joy. I thank God that I am the young woman he entrusted to preserve the mountain people's rich history. I am blessed beyond measure!

Introduction

A crazy quilt is made from a patchwork of irregular-shaped pieces of fabric that are sewn together with various decorative stitches and embellishments on each seam. Although lacking in a specific design, a crazy quilt's beauty comes from the randomly varying sizes, shapes, and colors of the different fabrics, bringing them together to make a one-of-a-kind comforter that not only brings warmth to the body but to the soul as well. Sewn with love, each cutout may have been taken from someone's favorite piece of worn-out clothing or perhaps a man's tie or colorful hatband. When finished, the quilt is a thing of beauty made from a mishmash of different things, thus creating an intricate fabric of our past.

In the same way, I chose *Crazy Quilt* as the title of the sixth book in the Backroads series, in that it is a patchwork of interviews, historical places, slice-of-life vignettes, and modern-day people preserving the old-time arts here in my corner of the world.

As I was tossing around the idea of actually undertaking writing another book, the title *Crazy Quilt* kept going through my head. I prayed, asking God to somehow confirm whether or not this was a worthwhile project. Lying in bed one night, I began thinking about what type of cover would go with the title and also compliment the other five Backroads books about Appalachian life. I remembered that my mother-in-law, Annie Coffey, had had a bunch of quilts. We had inherited them after she passed. The next morning, I got up and looked through an armoire where the quilts are kept. Lo and behold, there was a very old quilt with a colorful patchwork of cloth pieces and intricate hand-sewn embroidery holding it together. I spread the quilt on the floor, got out my camera, and snapped a few pictures to see if it would make a viable front cover.

I didn't look closely at the embroidered sayings stitched on the cloth until I enlarged the photos on my computer. There, in the center of the quilt, was a piece of pink dotted material with the initials D.F.G. stitched in pink. Underneath the initials something else was written. Imagine my complete shock as I stared at the written message the sewer had stitched, most likely in the early 1900s. It said, "Crazy Quilt." What are the chances that that particular name would suddenly pop into my head for a book title, accompanied by a front cover photograph of an antique quilt that was made over a hundred years ago? Some may call it an eerie coincidence, but I believe it was God giving me the sign I needed to begin work on the book you are holding in your hand.

The back cover shows four of the mountain women I've interviewed over the years who sewed quilts. They made them for their families, not only for warmth but also for beauty and self-expression. At top left is LaRue Fauber Wilson of Raphine with Lorean Falls Painter of Raphine on the right. At bottom left is Mabel Truslow Napier of Spruce Creek and Lura Coffey Steele of Steeles Tavern next to her. Like the quilts the ladies have created, this book represents a piece of the past that cannot be replicated. Separately, the stories in *Crazy Quilt* are interesting in themselves; but put together as a whole, they create a beautiful picture of what Virginia's Southern Highlands and their people are all about.

Introduction

Read about Steve Bridge's country grocery, carrying 1900's replicas of the various items everyday folk needed to make life a little easier in an earlier century. The store, which was built next to Steve's home, contains everything from pitchforks to chewing tobacco, garden seeds to chamber pots. Walking through the door instantly takes you back to a simpler time when neighbors came in for what they needed and left with a bit of gossip and a slice of rat cheese on a cracker.

Learn about the Dodd Cabin, a humble log dwelling that was built in the village of Beech Grove in the early 1900s and is intact today thanks to the Mansfield family, who bought and preserved it for the next generation. The cabin is open to visitors on Sunday afternoons, and the Mansfields host a Christmas Eve community get-together complete with hot mulled cider, finger foods, and carol singing. Natural decorations, candles in the windows, and a blazing fire in the fireplace welcome those looking for a nostalgic way to spend the night before Christmas.

Watch Kay Campbell revive the primitive art of painting floorcloths that are beautiful as well as functional alternatives to carpeting. Floorcloths were used in the White House by many early US presidents, and Thomas Jefferson had a number of them gracing the floors of his beloved Monticello. Today, floorcloths are every bit as useful as they were in earlier times and fit in with any type of décor and color scheme.

Meet the Reinhardts, Max and Sylvia, who bought the run-down train depot in Lyndhurst, lovingly restored the historical structure, and made it their unique home. Sylvia's artwork is abundant both inside and outside the depot, and Max's woodworking skills add to the nostalgic beauty of an earlier time.

The Blue Ridge Mountains teem with myriad histories that need to be documented, and *Crazy Quilt* is filled with as many of these stories as I could fit between two covers. I talked with people who continue to preserve many of the old arts, such as soap making, chair caning, and restoring log cabins to their original beauty. There are local landmarks, such as Woodson's Mill (still grinding grain); early homes, churches, and cabins from the late 1700s into the 1800s; and many of my unpublished "slice-of-life" vignettes about everyday living that folks seem to enjoy. And, of course, no Backroads book would be complete without interviews with the elder mountain people who make yesterday come alive with their oral histories. It is my wish that you enjoy them all through the pages of *Crazy Quilt*.

Crazy Quilt

Woodson's Mill in Lowesville, Virginia

1

Woodson's Mill, Lowesville

Back in the early 1970s, while visiting the mountains and riding the back roads, I came upon an abandoned mill in Lowesville. I got out and took a photograph of it. Not being from the area, until I later moved here, I never knew the name of the old mill or the history of its early beginnings.

The mill in the 1970s, before restoration

I met a man by the name of Chris Anderson, who is really into the early histories of Virginia's grist mills and has written many articles for the *Old Mill News* magazine. The first part of the Woodson's Mill article has been taken from the spring 1987 edition of the magazine that was co-written by Chris and former owner of the mill, J. Gill Brokenbrough Jr. It gives a concise and accurate description of Woodson's Mill from its beginning until the present time. It is with permission that I'd like to include it, along with interviews with Will Brokenbrough, son of former owner, Gill, and now present owner of the old mill property; Steve Roberts, millwright; and David Woodson (Dr. Woodson's grandson), mill docent.

The men of the mill: Will, Steve, and David

A few short years ago, Woodson's Mill was one of the too many dilapidated-and-dying Virginia water mills. Since 1972, when first we learned of its existence, my colleagues and I have watched this once-proud, four-story structure slump further and further into decline with each visit. Now the old mill has new life and breath again—the only one of its kind operating in Nelson County, and one of the few double overshot grist mills in the nation. Regrettably, five other mills still standing in this same area are fast following the path that, until recently, Woodson's Mill had trod.

Originally constructed in 1794 by Guiliford Campbell, the mill was rebuilt in 1845 and then purchased in 1900 by Dr. Julian B. Woodson. "Doc Woodson's Old Mill," as it was referred to locally, became an industrial center through expansion and modernization that began in 1904.

Through the years, flour and cornmeal, feed, lumber, cider, and ice were all produced at Woodson's. Across the road from the main complex were a stable and foundry and, later, a steam-powered sawmill. Woodson also owned a three-thousand-tree apple orchard, a 650-acre farm, and a machine shop—all on the mill property.

Today, the mill has two overshot wheels; but in Woodson's time, a third operated the sawmill and, later, the ice plant. The foundation for a fourth wheel, whose use is now unknown, also stands in a creek that runs through the property.

Following the death of Dr. Woodson in 1963, the mill lay idle for three years; the wooden teeth having been stripped from the main gear by an inexperienced successor to longtime miller Edd Willis. To repay a loan from Dr. Woodson, Willis, as a young man, went to work as a miller, and there he remained for sixty years.

In 1966, Huron T. Campbell purchased the mill property, using the smaller wheel to pump water to his reservoir. Over the years a number of people offered to buy the mill machinery, but the far-sighted Mr. Campbell always refused, hoping that a subsequent owner might restore the place.

In 1983, J. Gill Brokenbrough, Jr., of Norfolk, Virginia, hired Steve Roberts of Massie's Mill to paint the roof at

Early miller, Edd Willis

Woodson's. Steve then suggested clearing years of accumulated junk from the building and doing a general clean up. Practically before they knew it, Gill and Steve had made the decision to proceed with a total restoration. Prior to this, the dam, which is on the Piney River, had been prefabricated (poured all the way to the bedrock), and the race was cleared to allow water to again enter the three-acre pond, which lies downhill from the imposing stone house which is the property residence.

Steve and a crew of three went to work putting up new wood siding, replacing windows, and installing a new sill at the east end of the mill, thus averting an imminent collapse of that wall. Persimmon wood was used to fashion new teeth for the stripped main gear, and the two runs of stones and housings were cleaned and dressed like new. The roller mills, which were cleaned for display, would not be used as part of the mill operation.

One of the biggest problems was refurbishing the 12.5-by-8-foot Fitz overshot wheel, the lower third of which was virtually destroyed by water that had backed up in the tail race. To further complicate things, the header tank and flume were completely gone.

Gill had the wheel sent to a firm in Lynchburg, Virginia, where it was, for all intents and purposes, completely rebuilt along the design of the old Fitz wheel. A Norfolk firm, using old photographs and drawings as guidelines, fabricated the header tank and metal flume.

The smaller wheel at the west end of the building (a copy of a Fitz that the shrewd doctor thought too

Steve Roberts, millwright

expensive to buy) was built at Woodson's Foundry. Although a pipe carried water to the wheel, a header tank was added to allow control of the water flow from inside the mill. Keeping to tradition, this header tank was built by the miller and helpers in the mill workshop. This wheel is now operating and is used to generate electricity.

Concrete poured into the original stone-lined race carries the water flow from the picturesque pond to each end of the mill. The double tail race, in turn, carries it under Route 778 and back into the Piney River just below Lowesville.

What experts informed Gill Brokenbrough would require ten years to accomplish has instead taken only three—largely, he insists, thanks to the untiring efforts of Steve Roberts. Their wish is to have not only a restored mill as a museum, but to have a living, working mill, usefully providing service as it has for nearly two hundred years.

Dr. Julian Woodson

Dr. Julian B. Woodson was an intelligent, industrious man who had many talents and used them wisely throughout his life. In 1899, he graduated as president of his class at Washington University School of Medicine in St. Louis, Missouri. After graduation, he went to work for the Bureau of Pensions in Washington, DC, which was the agency that provided pensions for federal employees before Social Security came into being. In 1900, he became the owner of the former Piney River Mill in Lowesville, Virginia, and it became known thereafter as Woodson's Mill. Woodson had a doctor's office in a room off the main floor of the mill where he was the community's family practitioner; he did his share of dentistry as well as veterinarian work when needed.

He was elected to Virginia's senate and represented both Nelson and Amherst Counties from 1920 to 1938. He also served as chairman of the Agriculture, Mining, and Manufacturing Committee and on the Roads and Internal Navigation Committee. While on the latter, he was instrumental in improving roads in the state of Virginia along with his own district. He later served as medical examiner and superintendent of the Piedmont Sanitorium at Burkeville, which was a tuberculosis sanitorium for African Americans.

David Woodson, son of David Belmont Woodson and Aileen Hammersmith Woodson, was Dr. Julian Woodson's grandson, and he recalls his early years of spending the summers with his grandparents and what life was like around the mill at that time.

David Woodson, Dr. Woodson's grandson

David's grandfather was born and raised in the Lowesville area, and many of his relatives lived and operated businesses there. David's great-grandfather, David Staples Woodson, who fought in the Civil War, had a brother named Jake, who ran a country store in Lowesville where the present River View Market is located. Jake wanted to go back to farming, so he sold the store to his brother, who was not only the store's proprietor but also became the postmaster for the next forty years.

David was about nine years old when he started going to stay with his grandparents during the summer months. His grandmother, Rose Gilbert Woodson, ran the everyday activities of the farm and mill, along with miller Edd Willis, while Dr. Woodson was off attending to his many other obligations. David remembers her as being a very sharp woman who knew how to manage things in her husband's absence. She died in November 1954 at eighty-four years of age. The mill closed in 1957, and Dr. Woodson stayed on with the help of his housekeeper, Rosa Stevens, until 1959. Then, because of ongoing health problems, he went to live in a nursing facility in Richmond where he died in 1963.

David remembers his grandfather's medical practice as being a small room adjoining the mill office, outfitted with a day bed and all kinds of bottles full of pills. He didn't recall many people coming in for treatment there, because those were the days when doctors made house calls.

Dr. Woodson had the rock home adjacent to the mill constructed in 1929 by local builder, John Herbert Kurt Jr. David's father and a friend, who lived in Chicago at the time, came down for several weeks that summer, gathered river rocks in a horse-drawn wagon, and hauled them to the building site for the stonemason. David said the walls in the home are several feet thick. After his grandparents died, David and his cousin Julian came up and painted the inside of the house, which had a stucco finish, and David laughs at the memory of the stucco walls eating up the paint. "We put thirty-five gallons of paint on it and didn't finish!"

John H. Kurt Jr., born in 1881, was of German ancestry, but because of anti-German sentiment during the times the United States was at war with that country, John was also referred to as a John J. Kirt, Jack Kirt, and Jack Kirk. He is remembered today for his work as a builder of arts-and-crafts style houses, using rocks (also known as "river jacks")

The rock house, Will's present home

from local rivers. He built homes for several prominent families in Nelson County, including Doctor Herbert Dickie; Guy Miller, who was an elder at Massies Mill Presbyterian Church; Doctor Herman Clarke; Captain Billy Massie; as well as Doctor Julian Woodson. He was a talented carpenter and stonemason and was a generous and loving family man. He died on January 30, 1949, at the age of sixty-eight and will always be remembered for his legacy of stonework in the Nelson County, Virginia, area.

When David Woodson was asked if, as a child, his grandfather had let him work in the mill, David laughed and said, "No, I played in the mill! I was either playing or swimming in the lake. The lake wasn't there when Grandfather bought the property but was added later. They dug it out using teams of horses hooked to metal pans to scoop the dirt out. They lined the bottom with clay, and that became the reservoir for the mill. Before they would let me go to the lake, I had to learn to swim in the mill race, which was only so high, but I managed enough that they allowed me to swim the lake."

The mill race

Water came from the lake into the mill race, where it was funneled over the Fitz overshot wheel, which had been manufactured in Hanover, Pennsylvania. Earlier wheels were probably made of wood, but in the 1840s, modernization with steel products were becoming popular, and that's probably when it was replaced.

The original use for the smaller water wheel on the opposite end of the mill was to generate electricity for the mill and the house, since electricity had not come to the Lowesville area at that time. Dr. Woodson had a thirty-two-volt Dynamo generator and a bank of batteries in the house and the mill that were powered by water. He made a trip to the Fitz Company to get a price to make the size wheel he wanted, but he felt it was too expensive, so he came home and built one himself. He also piped water from a spring down to the mill, and the water emptied into a four-foot by eight-foot tank with no top. The wheel would turn and drive a piston pump, feeding water back up to a reservoir located behind the house. At a time when no one had indoor plumbing, the Woodson's were way ahead of the crowd.

The overshot Fitz waterwheel

In 2003, David moved to a farm about five miles away from Lowesville. Will Brokenbrough reopened Woodson's Mill in 2012, and David became a vital part of the operation, coming in to grind, make repairs, and act as a docent on Saturdays, when the mill is open to the public from 10:00 a.m. to 4:00 p.m. A docent is a person who leads tours or gives interpretive talks to those visiting a museum, art gallery, or, in this case, a working grist mill. David was also kind enough to give a brief account and photographs of how grain is ground once it comes to the mill.

Grain is brought in and dumped into a hole in the floor that leads to a wooden cone-shaped hopper that goes to the bottom of a bucket elevator. This then takes the grain upstairs and deposits it into a large metal silo.

The bucket elevator

The upstairs grain silo

Wooden grain hopper

Corn coming down the "sock," filling the hopper

From the silo, grain is chuted down to a second-floor wooden hopper that, in turn, feeds it into a long fabric sock that empties into another hopper. David designed the removable sock to self-feed the grain into a waiting hopper and to keep it from splattering out onto the floor. It also eliminates much of the dust associated with grinding.

The grain drops to a trough called a "shoe," which is shaken by a vertical wooden rod called the "damsel" that wobbles the shoe back and forth, shaking the kernels downward into the eye of the runner stone. A bottomless bucket is positioned around the damsel to keep the grain from jumping out on the top of the stone; instead directing it down between the two stones where it is ground.

Grain dropping to the "damsel"

The bed stone is fixed and doesn't move. It measures around eight inches thick and fifty inches in diameter. The top stone, called the runner stone, is the one that turns, and both stones have grooves and furrows for grinding. The runner stone can be raised and lowered for different textures, like fine or coarse. As the top stone rotates, the grain gets cracked in the middle of the two stones and is pushed to the outside by the spoke-like pattern of grooves. Everything done to this point is accomplished with water power. When the millstones need to be cleaned, sharpened, or repaired, the runner stone is lifted with a hand-powered stone crane. When the stones need to be redressed, the process takes about twenty-four hours for each one.

Once ground, the grain comes out of the chute and down to the floor, where it is picked up, sent up a shaft, and through the side of a metal cyclone. Inside, it swirls around until the grain falls out the bottom and goes to a sifter, while the top pipe carries excess air out a window.

The metal cyclone

The sifter has boxes with different sizes of screen wire inside that, contrary to thinking, sifts the fine meal on the top and the coarse at the bottom. Each box is for different things; corn, wheat, or buckwheat. In the photograph, corn was being ground, and the four bags contained grits, corn meal, flour, and bran (which is sold to hog farmers as a supplement).

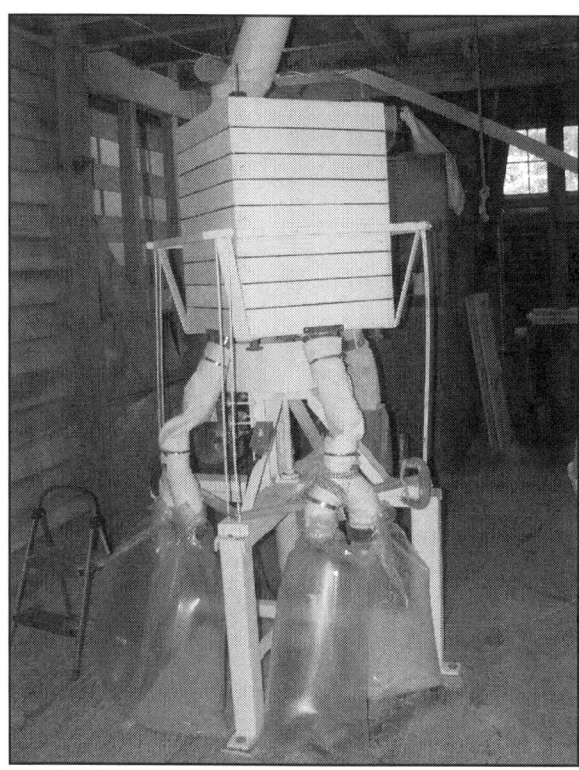

The sifter

After the meal is bagged, it goes into the cooler; from there, it goes to a bagging area where Will weighs and fills one-pound paper bags with the Woodson Mill insignia on the front and heat seals them shut. The product is sent to a distributor in Charlottesville and sold to stores in Virginia, where it can be purchased by the general public. It can also be bought at the mill or ordered online.

The cooler where grain is kept

J. Gill Brockenbrough Jr. owned and operated the family coffee business (First Colony Coffee & Teas and the James G. Gill Company) in Norfolk, Virginia, that was started by his great-grandfather and had been in existence since 1902. In the 1970s, Gill launched a line of imported coffee under the name First Colony Coffee and Tea Company, which became a very well-known and lucrative business. At that time, First Colony was some of the first gourmet coffee marketed in the United States.

When asked how his father came to find the mill, Will Brockenbrough, Gill's son and present owner of the mill, said his family was living in Norfolk, and at that time people were starting to buy vacation property in the mountains, especially at Wintergreen Ski Resort. Gill didn't want to live in a development. While exploring the back roads, he was drawn to a large stone house for sale in the village of Lowesville. By this time (1983), the mill had sat unused for twenty-six years and was in a bad state of disrepair.

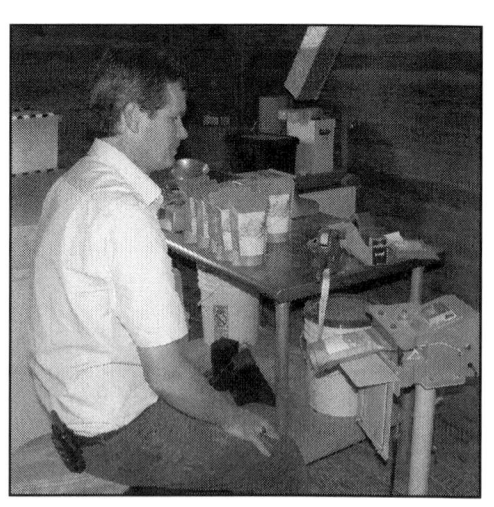

Will sealing product in the bagging area

Gill bought the stone residence, but, as for the mill, he said he wasn't sure if it was an asset or a liability. When he purchased the property from the Campbell estate, one of the relatives told him how close they had come to burning the mill down just so they could sell the house! The impressive stone house was used as the Brockenbrough's vacation home until Gill later moved in on a full-time basis.

In the fall of 1984, Gill hired Massies Mill native Steve Roberts to paint the roof of the mill to keep it from deteriorating further. Steve and his nephew, Peter Balin, began the arduous task of painting the steep metal roof, climbing on a homemade wooden "chicken ladder" that was hung over the ridge pole. Steve recalls that Peter was the first one up, climbing to the very top with his arms outstretched—to the horror of Gill, watching from the ground.

At first the men tried tying themselves to the roof with rope but found it too cumbersome, so they just stood carefully on the ladder while they painted. They applied a thick coat of fibrous black paint, first to one side and then the other, patching a part of the metal that needed replaced. The painting took about a week, and Steve was quick to point out that his nephew stuck with him until the mill was up and running smoothly; Steve said that he could not have done the work without Peter's help.

Once the roof painting was complete, the decision was made to tackle cleaning out the mill, which was being used by the former owner as a storage building and was filled with all kinds of junk. Steve said that he and Peter filled two enormous dumpsters with trash. Once the mill was cleared, Gill came up over the weekend from Norfolk and couldn't believe the interworking of the old mill's equipment that had been hidden under all the debris. Because of the foresight of Huron T. Campbell, the mill had been sold with all the working parts intact.

On Easter Sunday 1985, Steve hooked a hand-cranked mill up to the small wheel with a pulley. "It was Easter, and we thought it fitting that it was also the resurrection of the mill," reminisced Steve. "After that, I got permission to re-side the east end of the mill, which had deteriorated, and that's when Joe Mays and Phillip Campbell came in to help. Joe continued to work around the mill and was hired full time and later became the caretaker for many years."

As the re-siding was taking place, the large waterwheel, which was damaged from standing water and mud, was taken down and rebuilt by a firm in Lynchburg. While the wheel was being repaired, the old dirt raceway was formed up and poured with concrete, bringing water from the lake to the mill and over the newly refurbished wheel that powered the grinding process. Steve remembers that in earlier years, a local black church used the old millrace for baptisms.

He also recalls Gill's two mules, Elmer and Elvira, that Gill bought for show and to ride around the property. "He had a buggy, and he'd hook up the mules and ride up and down the road with other people who belonged to the Blue Ridge Harness and Saddle Club. Ted Hughes, of Arrington, was the president of the club at one time." Will said that the mules were brother and sister; Elvira was personable and could be ridden, but Elmer was the exact opposite. I added that you either got a "good" mule or a "bad" mule, and Will laughed and said his dad had one of each!

On May 12, 1986, a formal open house was held, inviting the public for the unveiling of the new waterwheel. Several later open houses were held, and Steve remembers that at one of them, by two o'clock in the afternoon, over one thousand servings of Brunswick stew had been served. "We ran out of stew for the last fifty people and had to serve them hot dogs!"

That same year, the mill became a Purina dealer; although the feed business never really took off, Steve said they had a lot of good customers who used the service, and "It gave us a reason for being here."

At this same time, the mill business began to pick up, and Gill, with his network of brokers, began shipping product to prominent retail stores around the country, including Bloomingdales, Marshall Field's, Thalhimers, and Macy's Department Stores. In 1987, a packing room was set up where cloth bags and liners with the Woodson's Mill logo on the front were filled and shipped out to distributors. Will said the cloth bags were somewhat of a novelty in gift shops, and people were more interested in buying the bags than the product. At that time cornmeal, grits, whole wheat, rye, and buckwheat were produced.

Today, people are more interested in the all-natural aspects of grain, and Woodson's produces both white and yellow Hickory King cornmeal and grits, buckwheat flour, whole wheat flour, Bloody Butcher (red corn) cornmeal and grits, three-grain pancake mix, and hushpuppy batter mix. They are currently working on a cornbread mix and all-purpose flour. The natural products are packaged in one-pound paper bags and vacuum sealed for freshness; they have no preservatives, bleaches, or chemical additives. For that reason, the various meals are best kept under refrigeration until needed.

Like David Woodson, Woodson's Mill served as the backdrop for Will Brockenbrough's childhood, and, at an early age, he developed a love of history and historic preservation. His father, Gill, continued to run the mill until he passed away in 2001. Joe Mays stayed on as caretaker for a time, but the mill eventually closed and was tied up in Gill's estate for four years until Will and his wife, Sarah, bought out Gill's second wife's interest.

Will was living in Savanna, Georgia, at the time, serving as an architectural history consultant, and it wasn't until 2011 that he and Sarah moved back to Virginia. Sarah, an Episcopal priest, was going to seminary in Alexandria, Virginia;

Will Brockenbrough, owner of Woodson's Mill

later, the couple took up residence in the old stone house. Will reconnected with Steve Roberts and together they reopened the mill for business in 2012. David Woodson became part of the operation as the mill's docent and has been there ever since.

When asked what they remembered and liked best about operating the mill, Will and Steve both agreed it was the older people who frequented Woodson's. Steve recalled, "Old-timers like Ed Massie, who was in his seventies back in 1986, came in and just hung out. Mrs. Campbell, who was then ninety years old, came to the first open house and cried tears of joy because the mill was, in her words, 'coming back.' George Woodson, one of Dr. Woodson's sons, would come up with his wife, Daphne, to get apples—probably from Saunders Brothers, since they were related—and he was the one who first showed us how to dress the millstones. He came up for a few days specifically to show us how to do it. We turned the stone over and set it up in front of him, and he went to work."

When I asked how the stone was dressed, Will said that a pointed hammer called a mill bill is tapped over the surface of the stone, giving it the rough texture needed to grind the grain.

Sitting in the mill office, where I talked to Will Brockenbrough and Steve Roberts on the last day of August 2018, it was clear how much the men respected and valued one another. Will called David Woodson the "mill ambassador," the one able to talk to people good-naturedly about the mill's early history, while he and Steve are busy grinding, packaging, and fixing equipment. Steve is labeled "head miller" by

Will, who said he learned so much about the milling business by just listening to Steve when he came to Woodson's as a young boy. Steve said with a smile how much he enjoys working with Will, the "proprietor" of Woodson's Mill, and how blessed he has been to watch it all come together and be a part of it all. "I'm just like a rabbit in a briar patch!"

Thanks to the Brockenbrough family, a bit of Virginia's rich early history continues to flourish in today's modern world. Woodson's is the only grist mill still operating in Nelson County, and Will believes it's the only commercially operated water-powered mill in Virginia. It was listed on the National Register of Historic Places by the Department of the Interior in 1992, and a more complete early history of the mill may be obtained from that National Register.

The historic Woodson's Mill

So in 2019, come by and step across the threshold of 225-year-old Woodson's Mill for an informational tour and to purchase some of its fresh-ground products. Hours are from 10:00 a.m. to 4:00 p.m. on the first Saturday of each month from May until September. Will, Steve, and David will be waiting to greet you.

Kay Campbell painting a floorcloth

2

Kay Campbell–Floorcloths

One of the earliest ways people covered bare floors was with floorcloths, which were first produced and imported from England by the Smith and Baber factory of London prior to 1754. These decorative rugs were used to insulate floors against cold and windy winters and, when heavy wool rugs were taken up in summer, to protect the wood from wear.

Itinerant stencilers created functional works of art for wealthy individuals, painting either solid colors or fancy cloths with borders. The basic procedure for making a floorcloth has not changed down through the years. Heavy canvas is prepared, and the weave is filled so that the cloth can receive

Popular Williamsburg pattern, "Bump Tavern"

the painted design. Paint is applied using block printing techniques, stenciling, or hand painting. The paint is applied in layers, then sealed. The result is a carpet that is easily cleaned with a damp mop; tough enough to withstand dogs, children, and furniture; and customizable in a wide variety of patterns ranging from historic to contemporary.

Kay showing a country-themed floorcloth

It is known that at least three United States presidents had floorcloths in their inventories. George Washington purchased one from Roberts and Company in 1796. Thomas Jefferson had at least two in the presidential mansion: one in a small dining room and one in the great hall. He also had several more painted canvases at Monticello. When John Adams's term as president was completed, a White House inventory listed a floorcloth among his possessions.

Kay Campbell, a Nelson County, Virginia, resident from the small hamlet of Beech Grove, began to get interested in making floorcloths after she bought an oriental rug and soon found her cats were always clawing it and shedding on it, making it hard to clean. Her daughter-in-law confided that a friend of hers had cats and had switched to floorcloths because of their durability. Kay had never heard of this type of rug, so she went online and saw they were rather pricey to

A Primitive Wool Company star pattern

buy. Instead, she looked at several sites that offered step-by-step instructions on how to make your own. Kay says, "I'm a DIYer [Do It Yourself] from way back and am a firm believer that if you have the right tools you can do anything."

Kay began making floorcloths in the spring of 2016, and in June of the same year, she retired from UVA after twenty-five years. Suddenly she had extra time on her hands, the perfect time to undertake a new project. Not that she needed another project. Kay and her husband, Carl, are farm folks with plenty to keep them busy, but Kay has always managed to self-entertain by doing all types of handwork, such as quilting, cross-stitch, crocheting, etc. During her research, Kay learned that floorcloths were originally made from sailcloth, repurposed from ship's sails that had been torn or damaged. Although these rugs can also be made from canvas, Kay prefers sticking with waterproof sailcloth, which she buys at fabric stores. She gives the following instructions on how she goes about making a start-to-finish floorcloth.

The first step in making a rug is to cut the cloth to the size you want plus a two-inch seam all around formed by either sewing or gluing. Kay was recently given a 1930's heavy-duty Singer sewing machine to do the stitching, but up to this point, she continues to use glue. It takes about twenty-four hours for the glue to set up, and the entire process of making a floorcloth, regardless of size, takes about two weeks to complete. When the weather is warmer, Kay works in her outdoor studio, but during the winter months, she sets up tables in her basement.

The next step is to put two coats of paint on the top side of the cloth. Kay explains that the rug's bottom needn't be painted, since the sailcloth is soft and waterproof. "I use tan or antique white as my base coat, but any color can be used. A roller can be used to apply the paint, but I use a two-inch brush because I find I can work the paint into the cloth better. It takes twenty-four hours to dry each paint application, so along with the gluing process, three days are invested in it already."

Sometimes Kay adds a different color border on her base coat, and I was surprised to learn that she uses regular, water-based, indoor house paint and not acrylic on her floorcloths.

The different patterns on the rugs are made with stencils that are taped directly on the cloth and then painted over. Kay says that the hardest part of the procedure is figuring how to lay out the stencils so they match all the way around. For pattern ideas, Kay looks online and in magazines that feature early American and primitive décor, many of which sell those kinds of stencils. She has also begun to make her own, which are easily cut out with a wood burning tool and can be used over and over. She says that depending on how many colors are used in the stenciling process, it can take another two or three days to complete.

When asked what she likes best about her hobby, Kay responds, "I like creating different patterns and blending all the colors together."

When all the painting and stenciling are done, Kay applies five coats of polyurethane, which has an overnight

Kay painting on a pattern

drying period between each coat. When finished, the final product is a thing of beauty as well as a functional addition to any home. Floorcloths wear well and are easily cleaned with a damp cloth. People have reported they have had them in use for over ten years. Kay explains that if one gets scuffed after a time, another coat of water-based polyurethane will bring back its luster. About the only thing that will mar a rug is a bend or fold in the fabric, which will make a permanent crease, so one must be careful to keep it flat. Kay also

A beautiful black-and-white star pattern

recommends putting a piece of rug pad under the floorcloth to keep it in place and includes one with each purchase.

Kay's first piece was an ambitious five-foot by seven-foot rug that is still in use in her living room. There was excess sailcloth left over from the project, so she made her daughter-in-law a table runner for her birthday and a few other small rugs. A co-worker bought one, word spread, and soon Kay found herself making more and more for other people. As what frequently happens, a hobby turned into a small business. She enjoys doing craft shows and farmer's markets, and this year will

Kay's first attempt at a 5' x 7' floorcloth

be expanding to other events as well. In addition to her rugs, Kay will be offering a variety of table runners, placemats, welcome signs, doll house rugs, and coasters. She also takes custom orders for pieces with high school/college logos and different breeds of animals painted on them.

Anyone wishing more information about purchasing one of Kay's custom floorcloths may call her at her home: 434-361-9186. Prices range from thirty-five dollars for a small floorcloth up to two hundred and fifty for a custom five-by-seven area rug, which is quite modest considering how durable and long-lasting these rugs are.

Tulip-inspired floorcloth pattern

Many thanks to Nelson County's Kay Campbell for reviving this beautiful and functional old-time craft. Her floorcloths are sure to bring many years of pleasure to those purchasing them.

Robert and June Morris at their Afton home

3

Robert and June Morris

Robert said that he first remembered meeting us at Clemmon Lawhorne's pig roast over on Coxes Creek when he found out that my husband, Billy, was going to be the new preacher at Hebron Baptist Church, where Robert attended. One by one, we had met his extended family and found them to be warm and welcoming. He and June's two grandchildren, Cole and Maddie, became a part of our youth class at the church, and both remain dear to our hearts.

Together, the Morrises are a perfect pair: outgoing, humorous, and family oriented. We are happy to call them friends, and I am especially glad they let me interview them for this book, because they are doing their part to preserve many of the old-time customs that seem to be disappearing before our eyes. Many thanks to Robert and June for the enjoyable evening we spent together and the delicious meal we shared with them.

∽∾∽

June is the daughter of Ella Hester Matheny Fox and Elmer Samuel Fox Jr., who always went by the name Junior

The Fox Orchard, 1944. (L to R) Quinton Miller, Frances F. Miller, E. S. Fox Jr., a boarding teacher, and E. S. Fox Sr.

despite his six-foot-two frame. The family lived on the paternal homeplace called Whistling Fox Farm in Afton, where June and Robert continue to live. The farm got its unique name from June's father, who whistled while he was out working in the fields or in the orchard. "We could always tell where he was, because we could hear him whistling," said June.

Junior was a farmer, like his father before him, who kept cattle and made hay from the land. But Junior later added milk cows, pigs, and chickens on the 160-acre farm and planted a large orchard, growing apples, peaches, and cherries. He was a deacon at Hebron Baptist Church and was the contractor responsible for building the church. He was an active member of the Ruritan Club, and he started the Rockfish Fire Department, where he was the lifetime fire chief.

June said, "He was the smartest man I ever knew and despite the fact he only had a fourth-grade education, he had more common sense than most anybody. He did so much in the community. He was real good at real estate and bought up a lot of property in Afton and Waynesboro. He rented the homes very reasonable and encouraged people to save up their money and buy their own homes."

June said her parents didn't get married until her mother was thirty-six years of age and her dad was forty-two. Her mom, Hester, had been engaged to a man when she was in her twenties, but he lost his life during World War II. Hester had settled down and, in her mind, thought she would remain unmarried for the rest of her life. An uncle and aunt set up a blind date between Hester and Junior, and the couple began dating on a regular basis. It didn't take very long. One night, when Junior was taking Hester home, he said to her, "You know, we're not getting any younger, and I think we should get married."

Hester was the women's editor for the *News Virginian* newspaper when they got married, and Junior told her he thought it would be best if she didn't work, so she quit her job. They had their first daughter, Nita Hester, on August 24, 1956, when Hester was thirty-seven years old and Junior was forty-three. Two years later, on June 13, 1958, June Adah came along, and the family was complete.

The Fox family lived in a large white farmhouse on the property, but when Nita was four and June was two years old, the house burned to the ground. June shared, "It was in January, and it was an electrical fire that started in the room Nita and I shared, but it was early in the morning and Mama had brought us down to breakfast, so we weren't upstairs. There was no fire department over here, so they had to call one in Waynesboro; but by the time the truck got here, the water in the truck had frozen and our pond was frozen, so they couldn't do a thing but stand and watch the house burn down. We lost everything except a tea set that Mama ran back and got out of the house. That's when my dad saw a need for a fire department over here.

"We went to Lacey Miller's, who lived next to us, and stayed. They went to town to buy some necessities, because we didn't even have a toothbrush . . . nothing! We were fortunate enough to find a house close by to rent that the people had just moved out of the day before, and the electric and heat were still turned on. We stayed there until Daddy built a new house on the same spot where the old one had been. All the rocks came from an old rock wall that was over in the field, and this was the house I grew up in."

I asked June if she had to help with the farmwork as she got older, and she laughed and said that no, she and her sister were spoiled. "I never learned how to drive the tractor, so I didn't have to help get up hay! But we helped sell the fruit that was sold on the farm. He had a peach called a 'Fox's Special,' which he grafted together with an apricot so it didn't turn dark. He also delivered the fruit to area grocery stores."

Robert's family lived in Albemarle County but left there in 1967 and moved to the Rockfish Orchard area of Afton when he was in the tenth grade. Robert's parents were Edith Hudson and Daniel Morris. Robert said he got his work ethic from his mother, who was the "strongest and workin'est woman on the earth, and she believed that all the work was going to be done. She never told me but one lie, and I had to correct her before she died. I told her, 'Mama, you only told me one lie,' and she said, 'What's that son?' 'You said hard work will never hurt you, but it's nearly killed me!' She always had two sayings: 'hard work will never hurt you' and 'we need to look out for each other.'"

Robert was the fourth of ten children born to the Morris family, arriving on March 24, 1951. The ten children by order of birth are: Linda, Tommy, Mabel, Robert, Gus, Lucy, Chellie, Patsy, Joe, and Chip. Gus passed away in September 2017, leaving nine surviving siblings.

Nine of the ten Morris siblings with their mother

June met Robert on Valentine's Day when she was in a friend's wedding at Hebron Church; later that same evening, she needed a date for her high school dance, and Robert escorted her. She waited for him to call to see her again, but he never did, so she thought he wasn't interested. One day, she baked some cookies and took them down to where he was living. It turned out that he had been sick, and that's why he hadn't called. He ended up working on the farm with June's dad, and they got on so well that he'd call up and ask to talk to Junior. June said, "They'd talk about the cows, and I'd get upset because he didn't want to talk to me."

Robert said that Junior was like a second daddy to him, and they never had a cross word between them. "He was good as gold, and he was like that with everybody. If somebody didn't like Junior Fox, then there was something wrong with them," said Robert. Junior passed away in 1983 at sixty-nine years of age.

Junior and Robert at the farm

Before marriage, June was going to Madison College (now JMU), studying home economics and business. After graduation, she worked at several Leggett Department Stores in Charlottesville. She and Robert dated for about two and a half years before they got married at Hebron Church on June 17, 1978.

June's parents gave them a little two-bedroom house; while living there, their son Colter was born in 1981. After his birth, it was decided that June would be a stay-at-home mom to raise the children. Their daughter Emily came in 1984, and they bought a larger farmhouse for the growing family. Caitlin arrived in 1986, and youngest daughter, Morgan, in 1991.

The farmhouse was getting a little crowded with only one bathroom, and the decision was made to build a house on the farm, closer to June's mother. Hester wanted a smaller house, so they built her a one-bedroom, one-bath home across the road, and the Morrises moved into the rock house where June had grown up. Hester lived in the small house for ten or eleven years before becoming a resident at an assisted-living

The four Morris children

facility. She lived there for about a year and a half before passing away at ninety years of age.

June began working two or three nights a week for Princess House, which is a home party-planning organization, and Robert came home from work to watch the children. June was very successful during the twenty-eight years she worked for Princess House; she met a lot of nice people who became friends, and she won all kinds of trips and got to travel to different places.

In earlier years, Robert worked in the construction trade but also continued to farm. When the children were small, he logged with a neighbor, Frankie Neese, for about twenty years and later with Danny Stevens of Tyro for almost ten years before he had to stop because of a neck injury. He was out of work for over a year, and it was at this time that June quit her job at Princess House and went back to work full time: five years for an optometrist; later, eight years at a dentist's office.

Because of his injury, Robert could no longer continue to log, so he began working part-time at McDow Funeral

McDow Funeral Home in Waynesboro

Home in Waynesboro as a funeral assistant. June's father was on the board of directors at the funeral home and owned stock in the company, some of which he gave them. When Junior passed away, Robert came on the board to take his place, and five years ago he became the president of McDow and treasurer. This past year, June has also become a McDow employee and is currently the office manager. Robert is very good at what he does, and he says he loves it. He is a people person; warm and comforting at a time when a grieving family needs that the most.

Although all four Morris children live in the Afton vicinity, Emily and Colter are the only ones still living on the farm. Colter and his wife, Julie, married in 2001, and their twins, Cole and Madelyn, were born in 2004 and are the apple of their grandparents' eyes. Everyone pitches in and helps with the work associated with running a farm.

Another job Robert is locally famous for is auctioneering. He accidentally became an auctioneer about thirty-five years ago at a PTA meeting when his father-in-law told him to get

"Apple Picker" auctioneering

up on the stage and sell a few items the ladies had on a bazaar table. Then a neighboring woman who had lost her husband wanted him to sell some tools and household items, and

Smiles on the auction-goers faces

June with grandson Cole and daughter Morgan

Robert told her that he didn't have a license. She told him to go down and get what he needed so he could sell her stuff. So Robert became a licensed and bonded auctioneer and was off on another journey that has lasted many years. People love coming to his auctions, as much for Robert's humorous banter as the tractors, tools, and farm gates he sells.

June is right there with him, signing people up, giving out numbers, and taking money when items are bought. She also does the flyers and advertising before the sale. As the Morrises said, "There's a lot more to it than just jumping up on the truck Saturday morning!" In addition to his children and grandchildren, some of the people who help Robert with the auctions are Charlie Rorrer, Ray Ashley, James Bell, Herbert

Robert with a nice-sized turkey

"Nomad" Jordan, the Danny Stevens family, and Robert's late brother, Gus, who was his right-hand man.

Robert enjoys all types of hunting and fishing, but by far his favorite sport is bear hunting, one of the most rugged sports the men from the mountains participate in. When asked when he started bear hunting, June laughed and said, "When he started to walk, that's when he started bear hunting!"

Robert hunts with a group of men from Tyro in Nelson County, and, like all bear hunters, he has a nickname. His is "Apple Picker," and I believe I knew him as such before I knew his real name. Others are Ellie May, Jethro, Pokeberry, T-Bo, Hollywood, Bulldog, Puddin', Bull Rider, and Butterbean . . . you know who you are!

A successful bear hunting party, 2007

The Morrises are a close-knit family, and all the kids and grandkids come to Robert and June's house every Wednesday night for supper. Despite Robert's constant humor, he has a quiet, reflective side, and anyone knowing him well knows what a big heart he has. He and June are kind, generous people, full of warmth and a strong faith in God. Robert wound up the evening by saying, "I've been surrounded by good people in my life, and you are blessed if you have friends, food, and your health!"

The Robert Morris family

The Lyndhurst Depot today

4

The Lyndhurst Train Depot and Post Office

The train station in Lyndhurst, Virginia, had a rich history of early service before its eventual demise. However, thanks to the restorative efforts of Max and Sylvia Reinhardt, the derelict building has become their unique private home, filled with mementos of the past as well as Sylvia's beautiful paintings. Read now about the depot's beginning and long career as a train station/post office and follow its history to the present day.

The Lyndhurst Depot, located at mile post 148.0 on the original Shenandoah Valley Railroad (SVRR) line, was a combination station and post office. It supposedly derived its name from SVRR's George C. Milne, who named the community after Lord Lyndhurst.

The SVRR (1867–1890) extended down the Shenandoah Valley from Hagerstown, Maryland, through the West Virginia panhandle into Virginia to reach Roanoke, Virginia, and to connect with the Norfolk and Western Railway (N&W). Construction began in 1870 and was completed on June 19, 1882. In September 1890, SVRR went into

An early photo of the depot (Courtesy of Augusta County Historical Society)

bankruptcy and was reorganized as the Shenandoah Valley Railway. In December of that same year, it became part of the Norfolk and Western line. Today the tracks are a major artery of the Norfolk Southern Railway system.

Gordon Patterson of Sherando served as stationmaster and postmaster at the Lyndhurst Depot for many years. In February 1969, a new modern post office was built just up the road from the old depot, and Gordon resumed his duties there until he retired in 1976 at the age of sixty-five. Marian Davis had been Gordon's part-time clerk at the depot from 1952 to 1969. After

Stationmaster Gordon Patterson, 1994

Gordon's retirement, Mrs. Davis served as postmaster at the new office until March 1, 1984.

In 1994, I interviewed Gordon about his time as station- and postmaster. He spent the first twenty-nine years of his working life as a telegraph operator for the Norfolk and Western Railroad and another twenty-four as postmaster of the Lyndhurst Post Office.

Around 1935, Gordon started his apprenticeship as a telegraph operator at the Lyndhurst railroad depot. He was twenty-four years old at the time, making sixty-three cents an hour. When he became an agent, his pay was increased to eighty-three cents an hour. He walked the five miles from his home in Sherando to the depot twice daily for a year while learning his trade. Telegraph training is a slow process. The ear is not naturally attuned to the clicking sound of Morse code, so it takes a long time to be able to send and receive messages with any speed. One who is proficient at it should be able to send messages as fast as one can type on a typewriter. Gordon laughed as he told me he used the "biblical system" of typing called the "seek and ye shall find" method!

When there were no messages being sent, Gordon helped the postmaster, Albert Finter, with duties in the post office, which was located inside the train depot. A year later, Gordon held rights as a telegraph operator from Winston-Salem, North Carolina, to Hagerstown, Maryland, on the Shenandoah Division.

The different shifts were called "tricks." Gordon said they consisted of three shifts from 8:00 a.m. to 4:00 p.m., 4:00 p.m. to 12:00 a.m., and 12:00 a.m. to 8:00 a.m. Gordon worked forty-one stations on the Valley line of the railroad and eight places on the Western line. He recalled, "You'd have to work as many days at each station as they'd want you to. You would ride the train to your destination, and the company would pay you time and a half for travel. We had codes we used over the wire that we understood, such as 'twenty-five on the wire' meant 'I'm busy . . . call me back later.' 'HR' meant 'hands ready' (I'm ready to receive a message). And '2-copy' always meant to make two copies of the letter."

Each station had a call signal, and the Lyndhurst station's was "HU." If another station wanted to call Lyndhurst, it would continuously tap "HU" on the telegraph until someone answered.

The Lyndhurst Depot, 1980

Because of all his early training in the post office, Gordon decided to resign from the railroad when a job as postmaster came open. On January 19, 1951, he became acting postmaster of the Lyndhurst Post Office; on June 30, 1952, he was appointed to the office. Along with his new title, he continued to act as telegraph operator, express agent, and freight agent all rolled into one. The Western Union was also located in the train depot, and one of Gordon's saddest duties was to hand-deliver casualty telegrams to the families of men who had lost their lives in the Korean War. He said that the government would authorize and pay for a taxi for as much as five dollars if the family was outside walking distance. He also remembered another sad incident when Levi Yoder was killed while walking across the railroad tracks and failed to see an oncoming train.

As postmaster, Gordon had to sort the mail and put it in people's boxes. The mail for people who didn't have a box at the post office would be placed on the carrier's desk, and the route carrier would sort it according to the boxes along his route. Mail to be sent to other districts was put into a cloth sack and hung on a metal hoop. It would be taken outside and held up so the brakeman could grab the bag as the train went by. Later, there was a panel of two lights that sat outside the station. When it was green, it meant there were no orders or shipments. When the panel showed red, it meant there were orders. A side track adjoined the freight office where the train could pull next to an unloading dock and take large items into the cavernous room.

Rural route carrier Andy Arnold

Andy Arnold received his first contract as a rural route carrier on July 1, 1909, delivering mail from the Lyndhurst depot—where it had been dropped by Norfolk and Western Railway—to the community of Love, where he lived.

Every morning at 6:00 a.m., Arnold carried the outgoing mail from Love to the Lyndhurst station. He would wait for the incoming mail, which arrived about 10:30 a.m., and take it back to the Love Post Office—a round-trip distance of twenty-six miles. He served 450 patrons, including boys and officers at the CCC Camp in Sherando. Arnold completed thirty-one years of constant service from 1909 until 1940; he had no vacation time and used substitutes only when he was ill, which was seldom. It is not known if he retired at this time or continued to carry the mail for several more years. Prior to Andy Arnold, there were only three other carriers: Peter Coffey, F. E. Campbell, and Columbus Hatter.

Although Andy Arnold was the rural mailman when Gordon started, it was Reginald Hatter who carried the mail once Gordon became postmaster. Gordon's finest compliment came from Reginald, who said, "It didn't make any difference to Gordon Patterson who came into the post office. If a person was a millionaire or a hobo, he treated them all the same." People responded in kind, bringing Gordon all sorts of gifts and coming in just to visit and talk with him. Gordon remembered with fondness two of his favorite "men of color," Walker Burden and John Vest.

"Walker had box number twenty-three, and he was just such a nice fella to talk to. John would come and walk down the tracks in the springtime and pick creasy greens. He'd come in with a big bag of them for me, and I'd offer to pay him, and he'd always tell me, 'Why you don't owe me anything, Mr. Gordon, but maybe I'll get you to help me fill out my tax papers when they come.' And I would, too!"

Gordon recalled that Tazewell Tench always had post office box number eleven from the time he moved to Lyndhurst until he moved away. "When we moved to the new post office in 1969, I saved box number eleven for him over there, too."

Lyndhurst in the early days was nothing but rural farmland, with houses few and far between. In the 1930s, when Gordon was still making his daily walk to the station, he said it was not uncommon to walk there and back without seeing one vehicle on the road. He said that Lyndhurst was classed as a "star route," which meant individual contractors could make a bid on it if they wanted to carry mail for that area. The lowest bid always got the route.

The rural route carrier after Reginald Hatter was Robert Monroe. After him, the route was consolidated with Stuarts Draft, and Homer Hinkle carried both routes. Years ago, a postmaster got paid by how many stamps he canceled in one day. The newspaper printed a list of unclaimed letters at the end of the month. If no one came to claim them, they were sent to the dead-letter office in Washington, DC, which would try to return them to the sender.

Gordon said, "Some of my fondest memories were of the schoolchildren who used to come in the depot while waiting for the bus. I used to jaw at them about everything, and if one morning I was kind of quiet, they'd whisper to each other, 'You better be quiet . . . Pat's a griping!' For the ones afraid to cross the railroad tracks alone, I went out and walked them across."

Postal hours were Monday through Saturday from eight in the morning until five in the afternoon, but many days Gordon Patterson went in at six o'clock in the morning. The office was portioned from the railway station with wooden pigeon holes for the mail slots. The building was heated with a wood stove that sat in the middle of the waiting room.

Marian Davis said the worst part of working at the old depot was that there was no bathroom, and she just knew the "Johnny house" out back was filled with snakes. She opted to walk over to neighbor Christine Floyd's house to use her facilities when the need arose.

Many changes have occurred since the early days of the Lyndhurst Post Office when Gordon was postmaster. It now

The early post office mail boxes (now in the Reinhardt's kitchen)

seems that paperwork has replaced people, and stress is an on-the-job given. Gone are the days when ruffled curtains draped the front window, and punch and cookies were served on Valentine's Day . . . and a man by the name of Charles Gordon Patterson had the time to hold a small hand and walk a frightened child across the railroad tracks.

List of Appointed Postmasters for Lyndhurst, Virginia, 1883–2019

Thomas M. Ziegler – October 2, 1883

John A. Stewart – December 28, 1883

Henry B. Sweeney – April 13, 1888

John M. Harner – March 28, 1890

Joseph A. Patterson – May 26, 1893

George W. Perry – 1897

A. P. Finter – 1897

C. Guy Wilson – July 1935

Charles G. Wilson – January 1, 1936

Orin B. Turner – April 6, 1941

Dorothy D. Turner – May 6, 1942 (acting)

Dorothy D. Turner – July 1, 1945 (appointed)

Charles Gordon Patterson – January 19, 1951 (acting)

Charles Gordon Patterson – June 30, 1952 (appointed) until retirement in 1976

Marian Davis – 1976 to March 1, 1984

Bruce Chandler – August 1984 to 1998

Elizabeth Berretta-Davis – Officer-in-Charge – June 26, 1998

Tsianina Barbara Baldwin – Officer-in-Charge – October 19, 1998

Tsianina Barbara Baldwin – Postmaster – November 7, 1998

Sandra L. Burnette – Officer-in-Charge – January 21, 2005

Debra K. Fitzgerald – Postmaster – April 2, 2005 (*Debra K. Fitzgerald's name changed to Debra Sue Kidd on April 20, 2005*)

Naomi Veney – Officer-in-Charge – June 28, 2012

On January 12, 2013, Lyndhurst Post Office converted into a Level 6 (6 hour) Remotely Managed Post Office under the direction of the Postmaster of the Waynesboro Post Office. The Lyndhurst Postmaster position remained until ultimately vacated.

Sonny Cubbage – Officer-in-Charge – June 5, 2013

Mandy K. Connellee – Postmaster – August 10, 2013, until present time

When the Lyndhurst depot was no longer used, the building was abandoned and boarded up. It was bought from N&W by Mr. Max Quillen and used for storage. As he was contemplating tearing the building down, a woman came and offered to buy and renovate it as a private residence. It was in a bad state of disrepair, yet she could see that the depot had "good bones." That plucky woman was Sylvia Leake, who had a vision of what the depot could be with a certain amount of "elbow grease."

Sylvia was born in Madison Heights on January 26, 1932, the daughter of Harry and Virginia Singleton. She lived there until the age of seventeen when her father took a job in Richmond, and she began pharmacy school at the Medical College of Virginia. There she met Max Reinhardt, who was in the same class.

A steam locomotive passing the depot, 1985 (Courtesy of Danny Hanger)

Max was born in Augsburg, Germany, on February 7, 1931, to Hans and Regina Reinhardt. The family was of Jewish descent, and Max's parents saw the antisemitism against the Jews growing and had the foresight to leave Germany with Max and his sister, Annalisa. A cousin, who was already living in the United States, sponsored the family, and Max was six years old when the family boarded a ship bound for New York City on October 27, 1937. An uncle was able to make it out several months later and lived with the Reinhardt's for a time. Everyone else in Max's family was lost in concentration camps during the Holocaust.

The Reinhardt family; Max is the young boy at right

Max's father, who owned a cigar and cigarette business in Germany, did all kinds of odd jobs in the US to keep the family afloat. Eventually, they moved to Richmond, where Max enrolled at MCV and met Sylvia.

After graduation in 1956, Max moved to Waynesboro and found work as a pharmacist at Standard Drug; he worked there for thirty-one years. Sylvia also became a pharmacist and was working at the Standard Drug Store warehouse in Richmond, where Max would call to place orders and talk to Sylvia. Sylvia next found work at People's Drug Store in Staunton and Waynesboro.

By this time, both had married other people and had families. Years later, however, both of their marriages had dissolved. Sylvia and Max reunited and were married on May 23, 1992.

The couple had not yet married when Sylvia bought the Lyndhurst depot in 1985. The windows were all boarded up, and the interior was full of old bags of fertilizer and an odd lot of litter. Max came to look at the building one night, and, with one sweep of a flashlight's beam, he said he thought that Sylvia had lost her mind. But she was not deterred and hired two local men to help with the cleanup. While this was going on, longtime postmaster Gordon Patterson stopped by. He was delighted when Sylvia offered him his old desk that was still in the depot office.

Once the place was cleared out, a wraparound deck was built, electricity was installed, partitions were put in, the walls were painted, plywood flooring was put down, and a bathroom was added. Insulation and new wood paneling began to make the old depot look more like a home. An upstairs loft was built, utilizing the open space of the freight room that had no ceiling. The railroad waiting room was turned into a bedroom, and the postal office became the kitchen, complete with the pigeon-holed mailboxes that the Reinhardt's left intact and now use as whatnot cubbies. Sylvia said that if there was one thing she would have done differently, it would have been to strip the many layers of paint off the walls down to bare wood.

Max explained that the railroad line was used not only for freight but also as a passenger line. Not many back then had cars, so people from the Lyndhurst community would buy a ticket and sit in the waiting room before boarding passenger cars that were pulled by an engine. They would ride to Waynesboro in the morning and come back on the three o'clock afternoon run. Gordon Patterson recalled that there were four passenger trains a day, and people riding the train paid seventeen cents for a one-way ticket.

I asked Sylvia if the train going by several times a day ever bothered them. She said no, that over the years they have grown accustomed to the noise and hardly ever notice it. She also said that because of the huge timbers the depot was built on, the house never shakes when the trains rumble by.

The Reinhardt's were married in 1992 at the House of Israel Synagogue in Staunton and rode to the reception at the depot in a 1930 Buick Marquette. They hired a band

Max and Sylvia on their wedding day

that played classical music at the wedding, as well as music at the depot. A dance floor was put down and guests danced the night away, "Until the mosquitoes came out!" Max said.

Max, who is the main cook in the family, baked and decorated a bride's cake and groom's cake (in the shape of an old car) for the wedding. Sylvia bragged on her husband, saying he was also an accomplished woodworker, electrician, and could do most anything else that needed to be done. "He is always interested in learning new things, and that is so important." Sylvia added, "And he's been so good to me."

Sylvia is a successful artist in her own right, working in mediums such as oils, acrylics, and papier-mâché. She paints murals, landscapes, and lifelike portraits and, at eighty-seven years of age, is still taking on work. She even sewed her own beautiful wedding dress. The walls of their home are beautifully decorated with her artwork, giving it a gallery feel.

The old freight room, now a living room

Several years ago, the Reinhardt's hosted an open house at the depot, and they said that about a hundred and fifty guests came, many community members pointing out the mail box that had belonged to them when Gordon Patterson was postmaster.

I want to thank Max and Sylvia Reinhardt, two of the most talented people I've ever met, for inviting a virtual stranger into their home and letting her write not only the history of the Lyndhurst depot but giving her a glimpse of their personal lives as well. As the interview came to a close, a freight train rumbled by the depot—a fitting end to a perfect day.

Max and Sylvia Reinhardt today

5

"New Shoes"

This is a true story that happened to me in the autumn of 1990 while living as a single gal in a rustic hunting camp just down the road from where I now live in Love, Virginia. It proved to be a valuable lesson in showing how God lovingly provides for our needs even before we ask.

Since it was late fall, I decided to cut the grass one last time before winter set in. I usually wore an old pair of grass-stained sneakers for this purpose, but that day I couldn't seem to locate where I had left them. I didn't have much luck finding them as I peered under the bed and in the closet, so I went outside in search of them. I was halfway out the door when the phone rang, and I momentarily forgot my tennis-shoe quest. As I hung up the telephone, a strong urge came over me to just wear my hiking boots instead of the usual sneakers. I argued with myself that the boots were too heavy and clunky to mow in, but the thought persisted, and I finally gave in to it and laced up my Carolinas.

Everything was going along fine until I decided to lower the push mower over a small bush in the front yard. I lowered the machine over the shrub and listened as it ground the leafless branches into mulch. I tried pulling the mower off the bush but found it had hung up on one of the larger branches that hadn't been chewed up.

It was stuck fast. I gave it a quick yank, and the mower suddenly came loose and flew toward me. Stepping backwards to get out of its way, I tripped over another bush directly behind me and watched in horror as the mower descended onto my right foot. The moment before impact, I sucked my toes as far back in the boot as possible and closed my eyes. When the blade hit, my foot went completely numb, and I figured that was all she wrote for my five little piggies. I had read somewhere that there is no pain when limbs are severed . . . just numbness.

Shaking, I hopped over to the front porch and sat down on the steps, afraid to look at my foot for fear that all my toes were gone and I was bleeding to death. I finally got enough nerve to look down and was amazed to see the front of my beloved boot chewed to smithereens but no blood pouring out. Calming, I slowly unlaced the boot and carefully inspected my numb toes that were turning black and blue by the minute. "Wiggle, wiggle"—all of them still worked! Immediately I thanked God for his still small voice that had told me to wear heavier shoes instead of the lightweight sneakers.

I began to lament my favorite pair of boots, realizing I had no money to buy another pair for the upcoming winter. But then I thought of what could have easily happened if I had found my tennis shoes; an outcome that might have had a very different and dangerous ending. Right there was cause to think how carefully God watches over and protects us. But the story wasn't over.

The next day, my daughter called and said something that made my mouth drop and left me speechless. Seems they got a new shipment of expensive, state-of-the-art hiking boots at the local outfitter store where she worked, and one pair had a slight defect that rendered them unsaleable. The manufacturer didn't want them back and said to just dispose of them.

"Mom," said Heather, "They are size 7 . . . just your size. I can drop them by on my way home if you want them and can use another pair."

That cool fall day I learned how God's tender love and provision is always available to his children . . . even before we ask.

Jill Bivens, soap maker extraordinaire

6

Jill Bivens– Soap Making

One of man's basic needs is cleansing. Native Americans bathed in streams, using witch hazel and soapwort to wash themselves. Early settlers found that lye leached from wood ashes, added to water and melted fat, produced a soap that could be used for personal hygiene and washing clothes—and, on occasion, washing the mouth of a naughty child!

Commercial companies offer bath soap, but there are many do-it-yourselfers who experiment with new and exciting examples of this basic necessity. Jill Bivens, a Nelson County native living in the Lovingston area, is a modern-day soap maker extraordinaire, and her products are not only easy on the eyes but excellent for the skin.

Jill began her endeavor in 2014 when her husband, Jim, suggested she find a hobby to combat the stress of a high-pressure job. Soap making popped into her head; she Googled the subject and found there was a wealth of information to help one get started.

Jill said, "The more I read, the more I thought, I can do this! When I made cold process soap for the first time, I bought a starter kit with all the necessary ingredients to make a two-pound batch of soap with a manmade scent of cranberry fig. Although I now use mostly natural, essential oils from plants such as lavender, lemongrass, mints, and Patchouli, I still like to use the different manmade fragrances as well."

Early on, Jill made "melt and pour" soap. A portion of a solid base such as glycerin, goat's milk, or shea butter is cut off and microwaved into a liquid; color and fragrance are added before pouring it into a mold. This technique allows you to make and use the soap in the same day. Jill now has her own recipes for cold process soap that takes longer to measure and mix and requires four to six-weeks of curing before it's ready to use. She said, "It's kind of like making a cake; the differ-

Measuring out the lye flakes

ence is making one from a mix and making one from scratch. When you measure everything out and mix it together, it takes longer, but the final product is what I call 'real' soap."

The day I went to talk with Jill, she was making lemongrass/charcoal/calendula soap and explained the process as she went along.

The kitchen sink was filled with hot, soapy water so used utensils could soak while Jill worked. A recipe for the soap gave the exact amount of oils and lye content needed for each batch. She wrote down the date so she would know when the curing time was up. Frozen goat's milk was used as a liquid base. Before lye flakes were added, Jill donned gloves, mask, and goggles to protect herself from fumes and splashes. She measured everything on a digital scale.

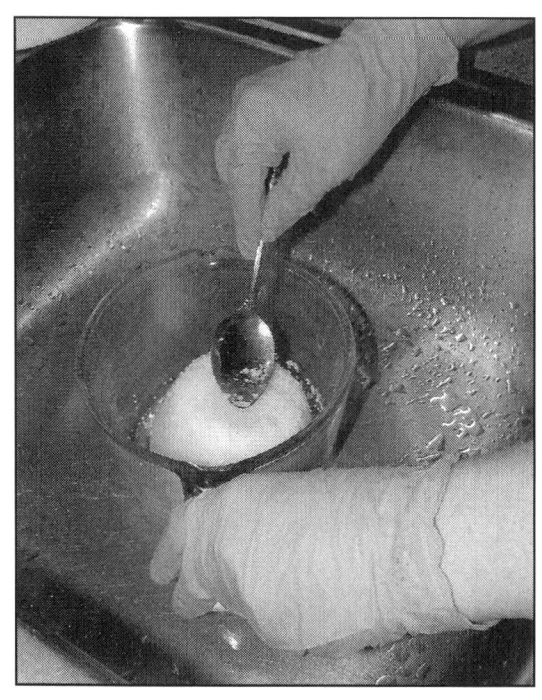

Mixing the lye and frozen goat's milk

Combining the lye mixture with oil

Blending with a stick blender

The three main oils most used in soap making are olive, coconut, and palm. Jill used those along with castor, rice bran, and almond oil in solid form. The oils were microwaved until melted. Liquid salt was added to the lye mixture (for harder soap), and this solution was added to the oils and mixed with a stick blender until thick.

Two portions of the soap were separated and activated charcoal was added, lending a dark gray color to the batter. Jill added dried calen-

Layering the soap coloring

dula petals to the mix, along with lemongrass essential oil, which intensified the fragrance. She then layered the colors in the mold. A wooden stick was pulled across the batter to make a pretty finished design. Ninety-one percent alcohol was sprayed on to help prevent soda ash from forming on the soap, which is a white film that creates a harmless cosmetic issue.

Sprinkling the calendula petals on top

The alcohol also helped stick down the calendula petals that Jill sprinkled on top. The mold was placed in front of a

A small sampling of Jill's products

Gift baskets, made to order

fan to help the soap to cool and start to harden; the process took about an hour.

After Jill had been making soap for a while, she had a large excess that she gifted to family and friends. Word spread, and soap making at the Bivens house began in earnest. An aunt asked what Jill was going to call her new venture, and Jill blurted out, "Fat Cat Soap Works," in honor of her six beloved cats. In addition to specialty soaps, she also makes lotions and body butters, sugar scrubs, lip balm, candles, and gift baskets.

Because she is a one-woman hobbyist, and it takes four to six weeks to cure the soap, Jill only sells at events that fit in with her busy schedule. She adds, "I am only one person making small batches of soap in my kitchen, so don't look for Fat Cat Soap products in large retail stores." But Jill's products are available at the Corner Spa in Lovingston, at Old Southern Charm in Colleen, and at many upcoming Virginia festivals.

Jill at a local festival

Summing up the interview, Jill said, "I'm not out to create a huge company. Making soap gives me the freedom to do what I want, when I want, and even after four years, I am still amazed when people buy my soap and say how much they love it."

Anyone wishing to get in touch with Jill to ask about her products and upcoming events may do so by phone at **(434) 906-7545** or through her email at fatcatsoapworks@gmail.com.

Slicing individual bars of soap

Stone wall at Humpback Farm on Blue Ridge Parkway

7

Stone Walls

Stone walls stretching throughout the Blue Ridge Mountains are part of the early landscape and were built by people who settled in the Virginia highlands during the eighteenth and nineteenth centuries. As they began clearing the land for farming, these people found an abundance of native rock that they used to their benefit. The

Stone wall at the top of Reed's Gap

rocks were gathered and piled into stone walls, which were a convenient and aesthetic way in which to dispose of them; plus, the walls could be used to mark boundary lines, family cemeteries, gardens, or to keep livestock inside a barrier while keeping predators out.

These fences of stone were all stacked by hand, carefully fitted into place, without benefit of any type of mortar or cement. They stood straight and strong, one stone depending on another for support. With heights taller than an average

Huge rocks at the Howard Brydge farm, Reed's Gap

man and widths up to six or seven feet, one can only imagine how many rocks were picked up and piled from a piece of new ground. The sheer size of some stones suggest that they were placed on wooden ground sleds pulled by horses or mules and hauled to the ever-growing walls, where they must have been put in place by several strong men.

These stone walls are still abundant in the area in which I live, whether located on the property of those still living here or on the homeplaces of long-abandoned farms, and are a visual reminder of the backbreaking work that went into building them. They stand as silent sentinels, a nostalgic tribute to the hearty Appalachian people who first settled here. The walls are part of a history that cannot be replicated and thus should be protected from the onslaught of progress whenever possible.

One of many rock walls at the Coffey homeplace, Chicken Holler

Those who have these early stone walls on their property are careful not to disturb them, and many native Virginians have a deep, abiding attachment to the walls, because they

Surrounding the barnyard at Humpback Farm

have been built upon family land that's been handed down over many generations.

Our own mountain land has been in the same family for eight generations, and looking at the graying walls that run serpentine across its ridges, one can only marvel at the hard work that must have gone into building them. By simply using what they had available at the time, without thinking of the future, the Appalachian people have unwittingly left a legacy for all to view and enjoy hundreds of years after their initial construction.

Stone Walls

Walls along the Blue Ridge Parkway

The Dodd cabin as it looks today

8

The Dodd Cabin, Beech Grove

Since I first moved to Love in 1980, I've always admired an old log cabin in Beech Grove that sat on a little knoll surrounded by a field of summer daylilies against a backdrop of blue mountains. I didn't know the early history of the cabin until 1989, when I interviewed Violet Dodd Fitzgerald Brownlee, who was part of the Dodd family who lived in the cabin in earlier years. The property is now owned by the Mansfield family, who bought it in 1973. The Mansfields,

The cabin in the 1980s

as well as Violet Brownlee, her son Cecil Fitzgerald, and area artist Linda Patrick, have provided invaluable information as to the early history of the Dodd cabin, and I wish to thank them for their part of this story.

The cabin was built between 1781 and 1800 and was a land grant from King George III given to a woman named Rachel Morrison in 1772. The land was eventually purchased by John Dodd. William A. Dodd, a family descendant, fought in the Civil War and also lived in the cabin. The following is William Dodd's 1931 obituary.

OBITUARY
OLD CONFEDERATE SOLDIER DIES

Beech Grove—William A. Dodd died at his home in Nelson County on Friday morning October 23, 1931. His death was not unexpected, as he had been ill for nearly two years and bedfast for about two months.

Mr. Dodd was born in 1840 on the same place where he died. He was 91 years, five months, and eight days old. He was a kind, loving father and a helpful neighbor.

Mr. Dodd was a confederate veteran, serving four years in the Civil War under General Robert E. Lee. He received not a wound during the war.

He was an active member of Beech Grove Christian Church for seventy-five years, serving as elder and superintendent of Sunday school; also a member of the W.C.T.U. for twenty-three years.

The funeral services were held from the residence Saturday morning, October 24, at 11:00 o'clock and conducted by Rev. J. M. Duckwall of Rockfish Presbyterian Church and assisted by C. F. Whitmore of Waynesboro Christian Church.

The following hymns were used at the home: "Have Thine Own Way" and "The End of the Road," and "Sometime We'll Understand" at the grave. His body was laid at rest in the Dodd Cemetery beside that of his wife, who died two years ago.

The following grandsons served as pallbearers: A. A. and Luther McGann, Jack Taylor, Layman and Martin Dodd.

The floral tributes, which were beautiful and numerous, were carried by granddaughters Misses Sue and Louise McGann, Charlotte and Margaret Dodd, Rachel Quick, and Mrs. H. T. Fitzgerald.

Mr. Dodd is survived by one son, C. W. Dodd; three daughters, Miss Emma Dodd, Mrs. Myra McGann, and Mrs. P. S. Dodd. Also, two daughters-in-law, Mrs. Hattie Dodd and Mrs. C. W. Dodd, all of Beech Grove. Sixteen grandchildren and twenty-two great-grandchildren and a host of friends survive. The sympathy of the community goes out to the family in their bereavement.

The earliest recorded ancestor of the Dodd family coming to the area of Beech Grove was a John Dodd, who came to the United States as an indentured servant to pay off a debt. He left Derbyshire, England, near Liverpool on February 11, 1700, on the ship *Lambe* bound for America. He was between the ages of thirty and thirty-four at the time of his departure. When his debt was paid off, he decided to stay and forge out a life for himself in the new land. In the Dodd family, there is an original sheepskin land grant from the King of England deeding 150 acres to a Rachel Morrison. A descendant of the above-mentioned John Dodd, also by the name of John, bought the parcel after he returned from the Revolutionary War.

In the 1761–1807 censuses for Amherst County, Virginia, John Dodd was recorded as owning the 150 acres in Dodd Hollow. He was married to Elizabeth Meeks, and their children, who were all born in the cabin, were: Susan, Alexander, Margaret, William, George, John, and Lucy. All four sons served in the Civil War and returned home.

According to Violet Dodd Brownlee, who was born and raised in the cabin, the homestead boasted a separate kitchen

Dodd family members

> This family was living in this log home
> when the picture was taken about 1926
> except for Violet Dodd and her two babies.
>
> All mentioned below were born
> in this log home
> except Margaret Ann Meeks Dodd
> and two babies.
>
> FRONT ROW:
> William A. Dodd, holding great grandson,
> Cecil Hersie Fitzgerald, Margaret Ann Meeks Dodd,
> Hattie R. Dodd, holding granddaughter,
> Joyce C. Fitzgerald.
>
> BACK ROW:
> Saylor Everett Dodd, William E. Dodd (Jack),
> Lewis S. Dodd, Margaret Dodd
> (all Hattie and Killian Dodd's children)
> Missing is Violet C. Dodd Fitzgerald,
> mother of two babies, Cecil and Joyce.
> Older woman in far back is Emma W. Dodd,
> daughter of
> William A. and Margaret Ann Meeks Dodd.

The caption that was provided for the above photo

house, a smokehouse, barn, springhouse, and chicken house. Originally, the cabin was made from chestnut logs cut from the property and chinked. As the family became more pros-

The Dodd Cabin, Beech Grove

Rock fireplace in main room

perous, the logs were covered with frame siding. The rock chimney was built by a Nellysford man by the name of Harris. Large logs were cut and placed in the wide fireplace to heat the home in winter.

Violet said that Lizzie Fitzgerald was the midwife who brought her into the world. Violet was the daughter of Killian Cornelius Dodd and his wife Hattie Rose Matheny Dodd. In all, seven children were born to the couple, two of whom died in infancy. Violet's family lived with Killian's parents. Growing up, she was especially attached to her grandmother and said, "I held on to her coattails everywhere she went."

Describing the homeplace, Violet said that the cabin was one big room downstairs with a sleeping loft containing four beds upstairs. The kitchen house was located to the front right of the cabin and was constructed of logs. She remembers it having a tarpaper roof and a stone chimney

The cabin sleeping loft

like the house. It was built away from the main house in case of fire. There was a large kitchen range for cooking and an eight-foot-long table that seated ten or more people. A large pie safe and buffet housed the china and utensils used by the family. A typical meal consisted of ham or pork shoulder and vegetables that the family had grown and preserved.

    Violet related that Christmas was always a very special time, and there was much visiting and eating with friends and relatives. Two of the biggest fall hams were cooked, and her grandmother would bake upwards of ten of her mouth-watering pound cakes to feed all the people who came to visit during the holidays. A tree was decorated with small bits of colored paper, and presents were exchanged among the family members. Violet recalls the scene of horse and buggies tied to the paling fence that surrounded the house. "I can see it just as plain as if it was yesterday, so many buggies. We were rich in food and rich in home."

Her mother was an excellent seamstress and made all the children's clothes. Violet remembers the little middy suit her mother made her to start school in. Violet walked to the one-room Beech Grove School where Edith Purvis and Laura Turner were teachers.

Music played an important part in the mountain people's lives. There was a tight rein kept on children back then, and parents didn't allow them to go just anywhere, so they had to be content to stay home and entertain themselves.

An early family photo at the cabin

"My daddy could play the violin so sweet it would make your hair stand on end," said Violet. "And my uncles, Walter and Woodie, played their banjos."

But the music was cut short when Violet's daddy contracted tuberculosis and died when Violet was only ten years old. "I remember him calling me to his bedside and telling me what a good girl I was," said Violet wistfully. "I thought I'd go crazy from grief when he died, but my Mama was a strong Christian woman who, with the help of family, raised her five children in a Christian home."

In the end, as the older folks died and the children left home, it was Hattie and Emma Dodd who lived alone in the cabin. They closed the door for the last time in 1955 to go live in a home closer to family. Emma Watson Dodd, born in 1866, spent her entire life in Nelson County's Beech Grove community. A sweet-tempered, single lady, she was one of the seven children of William and Margaret Dodd. William fought in the Civil War and Emma was born the year after the war ended. She loved children and wore a wraparound apron into which she gathered a misbehaving child with open arms and the kind words, "Come here child!"

Hattie and Emma Dodd

A quiet, retiring lady, Miss Emma learned to sew at an early age, and her nimble fingers stitched several quilts that are now on display in the old cabin. They were donated by Patsy Dodd Eye and Barbara Dodd Ramsey, the daughters of Josie and Martin Dodd, Miss Emma's nephew.

The name Beech Grove was thought to be given by some of the earliest settlers who came from England, since there is a Beech Grove near Manchester, England. It was typical to name the new settlements after the already established town of their homelands. The land in and around Beech Grove was cleared by these pioneers, and early photographs reveal the now forested mountains were once pasture fields and planted in corn.

People now pass the Dodd cabin on Beech Grove Road on their way to the Blue Ridge Parkway. In their eyes, the tiny one-room cabin is just a bit of nostalgia with an unknown history. But the members of the Dodd family still take the time to slow down and cast reverent glances at the old homeplace, savoring memories of a slower time when it was bursting with life. This story is for them.

Another part of the Dodd cabin history comes from the Mansfield family, who purchased the land along with the abandoned cabin in 1973. Robert Mansfield Sr. was a highly respected pastor from the Beech Grove community, and he—along with his wife, Eileen—started the Piney Mountain Bible Chapel.

Rob passed away in September 2014, but his legacy of serving Christ and others will never be forgotten. Eileen, along with her children, continues to hold services at the chapel each Sunday at 10:30 a.m., and all are welcome to attend.

The backside of the cabin

Rob Mansfield Sr. baptizing at the river

Restoration of the Dodd cabin started in October 2006. Ramsey Restoration leveled the cabin and rechinked the logs, and Vinny Valentino did the rock work on the chimney and the fireplace. The restoration took several years, and on May 31, 2008, the community was to invited to join the celebration of the cabin's completion.

The old log cabin now has new life, and during the spring, summer, and fall months, it is open to visitors each Sunday afternoon from 2:00 to 5:00 p.m. There is a community get-together on Christmas Eve; everyone can come and participate in singing carols, have a cup of hot mulled cider, and just enjoy the old-time atmosphere of an earlier era.

The Dodd Cabin, Beech Grove

The Mansfield family: Rob Jr., Merrilee, Eileen, and Andy

Steve Bridge (proprietor) inside his country grocery store

9

Stephens Grocery

Walking through the door of Steve Bridge's country grocery store is like stepping back to an earlier century when parents and grandparents shopped for products no home or farm could do without. Canning supplies, dry goods, pitch forks, soda pop, coffee, kerosene heaters, penny candy, seed planters, cleaning supplies, chamber pots,

An array of vintage products

sewing machine needles, and garden seeds line the shelves of Steve Bridge's replica of a 1900's store, bringing a wave of nostalgia to the Baby Boomer age group. Metal signs advertising Sunbeam Bread, Big Kick chewing tobacco, Kreemo Root Beer, Lee Overalls, and Snow King Baking Powder adorn the walls of the store, which is built adjacent to the Bridge home. Steve said that 99 percent of his collection is authentic vintage and antique items; there are just a few reproductions.

Rollback pricing for quality goods

Steve began seriously collecting about forty years ago, going to auctions and antique stores and looking for items that would round out a turn-of-the-century country store, never realizing that, in the future, his hobby would turn into an actual place that would bring a smile to the faces of people remembering a store like it from their youth.

Growing up on the family's small farm near Stuarts Draft, Steve said they were always working with old equipment, so he didn't understand the craze of people wanting to have antiques in and around their home until he graduated from Eastern Mennonite University and had a home of his own. After college, where he majored as a physical education teacher, Steve began his career in the recreation department at Woodrow Wilson Rehab Center, retiring in 2006 after twenty-nine years of service. While at the rehab center, he met and later married his wife, Amie, and credits her with starting him on the lifelong addiction of collecting things from the past. Both sets of their grandparents operated country stores, and items that were saved from those early businesses were given back to the Bridges by family members.

Steve's house and acreage, sitting high on a bluff looking out on Torrey Ridge, was built on part of the Frank Campbell property that adjoins the old Drawbond place. I commented on the towering oak trees surrounding the home, and Steve said, "Dad told me Grandma would bring them lunch from across the hill where they lived while they were working corn, and they would sit under the biggest tree to eat. That was in the 1920s, and the tree was big then."

The Bridges filled their cozy home with the early pieces they had, and soon other people began giving them things, too. Steve laughed and said, "We'd come home from somewhere, and there would be a bag on the porch with a note telling us to either keep the contents or take it to the dump."

After forty years of collecting and storing things in boxes, hanging them on walls, and hiding them away in closets, Steve began to entertain the idea of opening some type of retail store. There, people could buy reproduction antiques, and Steve would use his authentic pieces as decorative attractions, much like Cracker Barrel restaurants do. Between work and raising two daughters, that idea never came to fruition, but it was always in the back of his mind to somehow house the growing collection in one spot.

Three years ago, in the fall of 2016, Steve made the move to have a Byler Barn erected next to his house and designed it to look like an old country grocery store. "I wanted nine-foot walls so I could get that extra shelf around the top to put things. Because it was so high, the roof system had to be built later, after the building was put into place. From the time the crew pulled in, put the building in place, and leveled it up, to the time they left, was one hour. Monroe Chupp came to put the roof on, and Harry Devore and I finished the inside. We built the shelves, counter, insulated the walls, and painted everything."

To round things out, Steve bought an old National cash register for the counter. It was smaller than usual because everything in the store had to be scaled down to fit the space. The register is thought to be circa 1930s and only rings up to a dollar ninety-eight. On the shelf behind the cash register is a McCaskey account register that kept slips of paper with an amount owed if the customer didn't pay their bill the day of purchase but preferred to pay at the end of the month. Hanging from the ceiling is the scale Steve's great uncle, Ed Bridge, used to weigh sausage on after he butchered a hog; he would then drive his wagon to Waynesboro, selling the meat to customers.

Mountaintop grocery store

The oldest item in the store is a box advertising Pippin's Infants Fine Hosiery that actually still has a pair of socks inside. It is thought to be circa 1900. The newest purchase is a colorful cardboard cutout for Headliner Pocket Knives with twelve never-used knives attached to it.

Antique scale, choice tobacco, and rat cheese

Headliner Top Value Pocket Knives display

The inventory in Stephens Grocery is extensive and includes items from 1970 back to 1900. Bridge said the age groups most interested in looking at the collection are older people, remembering many of the products, and young children, who love the penny candy and crackers that are on hand. In later years, Steve plans to leave the store and contents to his two daughters, Jessie and Torri, so future generations can enjoy the nostalgic treasures of yesteryear that once belonged to their family.

Steve Bridge outside his unique grocery store

10

"Dating Myself by Metal Ice Cube Trays"

Well, I've officially dated myself as one of the "over 60" crowd, according a list sent to me by someone asking how many items I remembered from the 1940s and 1950s. Not only did I know every item on the list but also found a few more of my own to add. For this story, I thought I'd take all us oldsters on a sentimental journey that our children and grandchildren know nothing about.

Take metal ice cube trays. Although they were harder to get out because of the pull-and-yank method, the cubes were thicker and lasted longer in your drink, thus it didn't take as many. The silver tray made a lasting impression on me as a youngster when my older brother told me to place the tip of my tongue on it when he pulled it from the freezer. My mother had to extricate me from my frozen plight by holding my mouth under the kitchen spigot and letting warm water loosen me from its icy hold.

And I can still hear the liquid "gooshy" sound of the sprinkling bottle as my mom ironed clothes while watching the Arthur Godfrey show on Tuesday mornings. A Nehi pop bottle and a cork stopper with metal sprinkling head served to dampen the clothes long before steam irons came onto the scene.

If Tuesdays were "ironing day," Mondays were always "wash day." Our old Maytag sat in the basement, and I was constantly reminded not to get my long hair near the wringer lest it suck me in and flatten my head. Mothers have a graphic way of steering their children away from danger, and, let me tell you, it worked on me!

Remember the phrase, "bigger than a breadbox"? No kitchen was complete without a large, rounded metal box on the counter that kept a loaf of bread fresh for a week. I haven't seen one in use for ages, but you can still find 'em online.

And the gentle whirrh-whirrh sound the reel push mower my father used to cut the grass with is forever imprinted on my brain. Somehow, the noise of the later gasoline powered machines was just that . . . noise.

What kid born in the 1940s can ever forget the brightly colored aluminum tumblers our moms poured our Kool-Aid in? The glasses would frost with condensation, keeping your drink so cold it would make your teeth hurt when you took a sip.

A housewife's handiest cleaning tool was her trusty Bissell sweeper. Simple in design, its soft-bristle roller brushes swept up the flotsam and jetsam of daily living without having to drag the heavy Electrolux vacuum out of the closet.

One trip to the market would send us home with not only groceries, but S&H Green Stamps, as well. I'd paste them in the little books the grocery stores supplied and scan the catalogs for hours, dreaming of things I knew I'd never have enough stamps for.

My parents had a heavy black parlor fan that would cool our faces long before there was air conditioning. The wire cage on the front of the fan was missing after years of constant use, and my mother once again warded off danger by saying, "Keep your fingers away from the blades, or it will chop them off." The fan had to be retired after it inadvertently sucked a newspaper up from the floor and the wound-up paper stalled the mechanism and burned up the fan's motor.

"Dating Myself by Metal Ice Cube Trays"

The list is endless, but are you old enough to remember these? Blackjack and Teaberry gum, headlight dimmer switches on the floor, Felix the Cat, Roy Rogers and Dale Evans, home milk delivery in glass bottles with cardboard stoppers, telephone party lines, Butch wax, PF Flyers and Red Ball Jets, drive-in theaters, Brownie Hawkeye cameras, roller skate keys, Lifebuoy soap and Oxydol washing powder (with the big red bull's eye on the box), Wurlitzer juke boxes that lit up and played all our favorite 45 RPM records. If you scored high on knowing these, you just might be considered one of the "over 60" crowd. Welcome to the club!

Alice Higgins caning a chair bottom

11

Alice Higgins– Chair Caning

A few years ago, we found a set of chairs in the attic of Billy's mother's outbuilding that I thought would go perfectly with our long kitchen harvest table. They were a beautifully grained oak but had no bottom seats. About the same time, we visited the Factory Antique Mall in Verona, Virginia, and started talking to a woman who had a booth there; she wove seat bottoms. We clicked immediately, and she was hired to put splint bottoms in all six chairs. That was almost ten years ago, and they are still in perfect condition and have no sagging whatsoever.

Over the years, I've referred others wanting various types of chairs and rockers rewoven to her, and I'm happy that she agreed to let me interview her for *Crazy Quilt*, which features modern-day people preserving old-time crafts. As with any story, the road that led Alice to her craft is a winding one; but once on the right path, she found her niche and became a master.

Born and raised in Churchville, Virginia, Alice was a very active child. Her father was killed in a construction accident when she was ten years old, and she admits that athletics helped her excel in sports and her personal life. In high school, she concentrated on basketball and track. As a junior, she was the Virginia state champion for the high jump and was later inducted into the Buffalo Gap High School Sports Hall of Fame. She attended Radford University, where she played college basketball.

Before starting her chair-caning business, Alice Higgins had a number of different jobs. In the early 1980s, after graduating from Radford University to become a teacher, Alice could not find employment in her field, so she went to work in the prison system for seven years. Next, she became a mail carrier at the contract postal station on the grounds at Woodrow Wilson Rehab Center in Fishersville, Virginia, and worked there until 2003.

That same year, she married David Higgins. Their blended family had a combined four children, and they are currently enjoying their five grandchildren. Alice also had a part-time job with a furniture refinisher, and she found that she had an interest in learning the different types of weaves needed to restore chair bottoms. She made good use of the library, learning from books how to use various materials for each weave. Alice laughed when she said, "It was a lot of trial and error, and I did a lot of ripping out and figuring things out on my own. I started with the hand-woven cane and really enjoyed that, so I began learning all the other weaves, such as splint, rush, and pre-woven cane.

"When the man who owned the refinishing company retired and closed his shop, I kept the chair-caning part of the business going. In 2005, I established my business, Higgins Chair Caning, and in 2006, came to the Factory Antique Mall in Verona and set up a booth to get some exposure, and have been here ever since. I mostly do caning, but have expanded into also buying, restoring, and selling antiques as well.

"In 2012, I formed a partnership with Jay Russell, who has the booth next to mine called Valley Antiques and Collectibles. At that time, he had a table that wasn't selling,

Alice's sign at the Factory Antique Mall

and I had a set of chairs, so we put them together in my booth since I had more room, and the table sold right away. Our booth has Amish barn stars of top-quality metal that is crimped together and made from actual old barn roofs out of Pennsylvania. He's the one person who has taught me the most about antiques. Jay is what I call the 'picker' . . . the one who goes out and picks things up, and I am in charge of 'sales.' Jay has opened a ton of learning opportunities for me and provides ongoing entertainment."

I met Jay the day of the interview, and his booth is filled with antique furniture, lamps, trunks, machinist chests, and all kinds of interesting collectibles. He has a quick wit and had us in stitches while we talked. It's easy to see that they have the utmost respect for one another but enjoy playful banter back and forth on the days they are working together.

If an item is brought in, Alice tries to give the person a time-span to let them know just how long it will take her to finish.

Alice and her booth partner, Jay Russell

She says it's hard to know just how long each project will take. Judging by how busy she is, it may be several months before she can even start working on another chair. "Chair caning is very time consuming and exacting work, and I tell people an individual chair may take anywhere from five to twenty hours to complete." There are a lot of factors to consider, such as how a chair is put together and whether or not Alice will have to glue loose joints or do some repair work before starting the weave. The type of weave and material used make for a wide range of pricing.

Finished chair bottom with seven-step caning pattern

"Recently, my son Kyler has moved back to Virginia from California and has started helping me with the repairs and refinishing work. I will take on furniture to refinish but only smaller pieces, because I need something I can break down and maneuver easily by myself in my home shop."

The only type seat that you have a choice of materials for is what they call a "four-rail chair." Splint bottoms, which look much like a basket weave, can be used on this type of chair, and they have all sorts of material and pattern options. The splints are made from the core of the natural rattan vine, which is imported. Alice recommends an application of lemon oil or Danish oil from time to time to keep the splints from becoming brittle.

Two different splint patterns

Weaving cane, which is made from the bark of the rattan vine, is a hand-woven, seven-step pattern that gives an octagonal appearance when finished. For continued pliability,

Alice recommends putting a damp towel on the cane from time to time, leaving it on for thirty minutes, and letting it dry naturally. Prewoven caning is a lot less time consuming because it comes in sheets, but Alice said it's still not easy to work with.

An example of prewoven cane

Rush seats are made from twisted plant-based rope or manmade tightly twisted paper, which is what Alice typically uses. A coat of shellac can be used to help preserve rush seats when they begin to wear.

A rush-bottom seat

Wicker is one of the last types of weaves Alice learned, and she does repair work on pieces that need patching. She said once you've learned the basic weaving techniques, learning another comes easier. Because wicker has so many indentations, a vacuum cleaner is good way to clean it, or if it's natural wicker, it can be sprayed off with a hose.

Alice states, "I get people who come by my booth and see what I'm doing and come back with a chair that needs a new seat. I get a lot of referrals. The chair I am working on now came from people who live in Florida who were coming to a family reunion in Virginia. They made arrangements ahead of time and dropped the chair off when they came, and I will have it done when they're ready to go back to Florida."

Alice sells all kinds of weaving products at her booth, and several years ago, she also put in an extensive line of salvage and reproductions of antique original hardware, such as knobs and pulls, in high quality brass, wood, glass, and

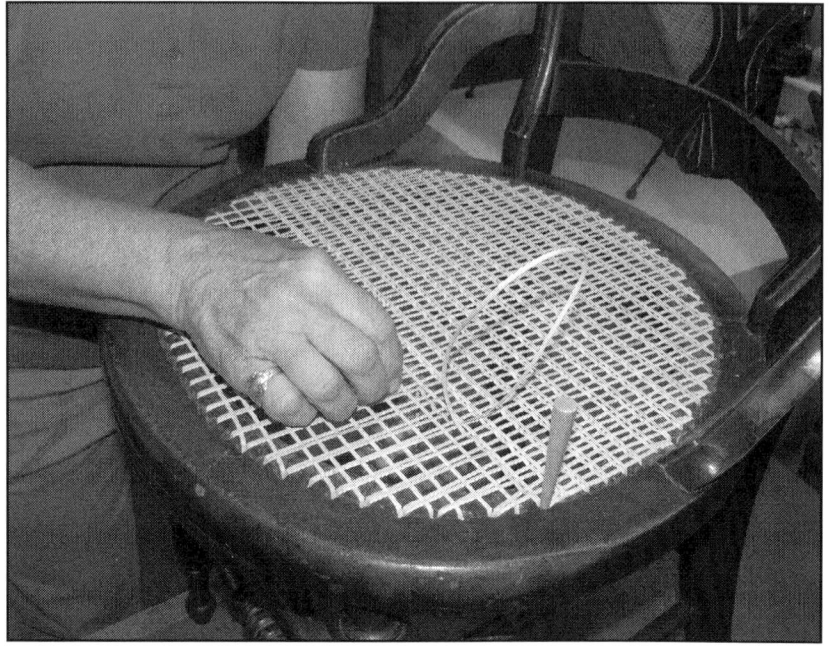

A close-up of the caning process

porcelain. She also carries Howard's products that give new life to older pieces without the hassle of stripping, plus a line of furniture care and cleaning products.

You can visit Alice at her "10th Street" booth at the Factory Antique Mall in Verona on Wednesday and Thursday from 10:00 a.m. to 5:00 p.m. and Friday and Saturday from 10:00 a.m. to 6:00 p.m. You can contact her via website at higginschaircaning.com, email her at higginschaircaning@gmail.com, or phone at 540-383-2854.

She also gives one-on-one individual instructions to those wishing to learn how to weave. If you don't have a chair, Alice will find one suitable for you to learn on. But if you have one of your own, the completed chair will be one that you, yourself, have put the bottom in.

Everyone has a talent, a gift that they enjoy and, if developed, can be used for the benefit of others. Alice Higgins's gift is chair caning, and she has learned her craft well.

A few of Alice's weaving materials

Gus, the "mystery man"

12

"Gus" (A Love Story)

Back in 1991, when I was a single gal, people assumed I had a boyfriend, because invariably my conversation was always peppered with talk of Gus. Since I didn't date, this was a hot topic at my place of employment, and my co-workers were always pressing for more information about where and when I had come in contact with this mysterious person. Being a pretty private individual about my personal life, I promised a story for the upcoming *Backroads* newspaper that I published about how Gus and I met.

When it came out, all the women were confused, but the men loved the story and guessed right away who this mystery person was. My brother, who lived in Florida, called me when he got his paper and wanted to know who actually wrote the piece, because he didn't believe I was clever enough to have written it. Nice vote of confidence, there, Bob! So, I am resurrecting the Gus story in *Crazy Quilt* for everyone's entertainment and also to give a little background information as to why I was so crazy over him.

It was just one of those chance meetings. He was standing in the doorway of an old garage when he first caught my eye. One look told me he was exactly the type I had been searching for, a little older perhaps but built solidly with a strong body. He had an air of unhurriedness about him, as if he liked being geared down to a slower pace.

I was attracted to him instantly and looking him over, I could tell he was in excellent condition for his forty years. I guessed he still had all his original parts, too.

I had all but given up thinking I'd ever find one like him, but not because I hadn't looked. There were a half dozen or so that I had been interested in, but somehow they lacked the qualities I had in mind. I wanted a guy with a strong character and a good family name. Someone I could rely on and go places with. I'd be proud to ride anywhere with Gus, for he's the kind that turns heads and people make favorable comments about wherever he goes.

I didn't want one with any bad habits; he couldn't smoke or drink the high-octane stuff. Gus seemed like a regular kind of fella who thrived on plain water and an occasional V-8.

He is three years younger than me and for that reason I thought he might be a little hard to handle at first, but I felt confident as we grew used to each other that I could gauge his moods better and steer him in the right direction!

I've always dreamed of having one who could really turn me on with nothing but his looks alone. And given the chance, I could turn him on, too. I held the key to make his engine race!

Oh, there would be times he'd probably act up, and I'd feel like throttling him . . . choking the daylights out of him. But when everything was running smoothly, I knew I'd end up loving him so much that if I didn't put on the brakes and quit clutching him, he'd end up exhausting me. Despite his forty years, he seemed never to tire.

He's the one I've had my heart set on for a long time. Now that I've found him, I want to keep him with me for the rest of my life. I plan to ride out life's bumps and curves with Gus, knowing that although he has his bad points as well as his good points, he's the type that plugs away and gets where he's going at a slow, steady speed. Yet, there is still plenty of spark left in the old boy, and when I run with Gus, I'll never be running bored or sitting idle, for that matter.

He's the kind that would wait patiently in a mall parking lot and never complain while I shopped all afternoon. For all these kind favors, I try and buy him presents I think he'll like . . . even ones I can't a Ford.

Gus will never be a Mercedes-Benz type. He's a plain old West Virginia boy with no frills about him. But he's dependable, even tempered, and a quick starter. More important, he brings a smile to my face whenever I see him.

He's a real '50s kind of guy who brings fond memories of my youth whenever I am with him. There's nothing quite like sliding in next to him, tuning the radio to the local oldies station, and listening to a little Chuck Berry as we cruise down the back roads together. Yes, the search is over. Since Gus came into my life, I have eyes for no other.

And that's the story of two forty-year-old classics that finally bumped into each other. Neither of us will ever be in the fast lane of life, but as the saying goes, "Getting there is half the fun!"

Here is a little more information as to why I was so enamored with Gus. As a child, I loved all things pertaining to an earlier time. Years later, someone called me an "old soul," which pretty much sums up my life then and now.

In high school, I met a boy who owned and drove a 1940 Ford Coupe (complete with rumble seat!), and I instantly fell in love. The love wasn't for the boy, however; it was his car I drooled over. When I finally got my driver's license and was starting to look for my first vehicle, the same boy put the old Ford up for sale for five hundred dollars. I *wanted* that car, but my dad nixed the idea, saying I wouldn't be able to find parts. The same was said for my next choice, a 1952 Ford truck. Being a compliant daughter, my dad's pronouncement of "girls don't drive trucks" wiped my dream off the bucket list. And so I went on to a newer, more respectable car.

After I married, the husband basically said the same thing, thwarting my idea of owning and driving an antique truck. Years later, when I was on my own and still driving the vehicle my former mate had picked for me, the said vehicle began to show weariness and wear. The kind mechanic who was constantly rescuing me from my troubled ride told me I needed to think about a second vehicle. I picked up a used-car sale magazine and there, in the "Classic Car" section,

The proud new owner of Gus

was my dream truck. It was only a year off . . . a 1951 Ford Flathead V-8, advertised in my price range.

I drove to West Virginia to take a look and gave the man a down payment, saying I'd be back the next week to pick it up. A co-worker, whose boyfriend had a rollback truck, was kind enough to take me over the Alleghenies to load up "Gus" and bring him back to Love.

My enthusiasm knew no bounds, and I must have washed and waxed the old truck several times during the first week I owned him. I began noticing how hard it was to turn the bus-sized steering wheel but just chalked it up to being "before power steering." When I rolled into my mechanic's garage, he came out wiping his greasy hands on a rag and said, "Please tell me this is *not* your second vehicle!" I assured

Lynn and Gus at their first Cruise-In

him it was, and could he take a look at it? I left Gus overnight and when I went to pick him up, the mechanic told me he'd had to replace a very worn part in the steering mechanism and asked, "How in the world were you driving this thing?" I replied, "Sheer determination!"

I went to Cruise-Ins, drove to work and up and down the mountains delivering the *Backroads* newspapers, happy as a clam. On my forty-fourth birthday, my co-workers at Waynesboro Hospital surprised me with a cake with a perfect picture of Gus on top, complete with dark red icing and the "51 Gus" license plate!

Riding the back roads with Gus

At one point, Gus needed a new paint job, so I talked a male co-worker into letting me use his large garage to single-handedly strip the entire body and sand it down to bare metal so several coats of the original "red vermillion" color could be sprayed on. When it was finished, Gus looked like a million bucks, and I felt like it.

When Billy Coffey and I eloped in the spring of 1993, we came back from our honeymoon only to find that our chil-

Lynn's forty-fourth birthday "Gus cake"

dren had filled Gus up with Styrofoam peanuts and balloons. Several months went by, and we were *still* finding occasional peanuts under the seats. When I broke my ankle one summer night, Billy piled the truck bed full of pillows and quilts, loaded me up in Gus, and drove to Hull's Drive-In Theater in Lexington to watch an outdoor movie. When my mother moved to Virginia, Gus was the only vehicle she could get in comfortably, because she could step up on the running board and slide in. When she had cataract surgery and had to wear wraparound sunglasses for a few days, I took her out riding, and she remarked that a lot of men were staring at her when they passed. I told her, "Mom, that's because you look

Lynn stripping the old paint off Gus

so cool!" She smiled smugly, and I never did tell her they were ogling the truck.

We continued to drive Gus and rode many a happy mile together for about ten years, but remarriage, children and grandchildren, jobs, and just life in general put Gus on the sidelines for a time. A friend came one day, took one look at the semi-abandoned truck sitting in the driveway, and said, "Ain't you ashamed for treating Gus that way?" To be truthful, I was. So I advertised in a car magazine, and the first and only response was from a man who didn't even need to drive Gus to know it was just what he was looking for. George was

A large project almost done

a three-time cancer survivor who wanted an old truck that he and his three grandsons could tinker on. The day he came to pick up Gus, I wasn't sad watching him ride down the mountain. I knew my old truck would have new life, making his new owner and those boys as happy as he had made me.

The present Jim Snead cabin

13

The Jim Snead Cabin, Fork Mountain

The old weathered cabin still stands proudly on a little grassy knoll deep in the Virginia mountains. It is now owned by John Farrish, who bought the cabin and five and a half acres in 2009 as part of the original 112-acre tract the Snead family owned. John was told the cabin was built around 1800, and he now uses it as a camp. The barn and large corn crib at the bottom of the property, along with the old cabin that has stood for several hundred years, make for a beautiful setting.

In the July 2003 edition of the *Backroads* newspaper, I interviewed Della Snead Fitzgerald, who at the time was ninety-six years of age. Della, who was born on a Sunday afternoon on July 28, 1907, grew up at the family cabin located on Fork Mountain near the hamlet of Montebello. Della passed away that same autumn on October 23, 2003, and I am honored to reproduce the original article by permission of her family.

Della was the daughter of James Crist Snead and his wife, Mary Elizabeth "Betty" Fitzgerald Snead, and was the eldest of seven children born to the couple.

Della at age three

A second daughter, Eva, was born in September 1908, and Della faintly remembered her as being a delicate child with blue eyes and blond hair. Eva died in 1910 at eighteen months of age. Della was not quite three years of age but can remember her father carrying her sister to the graveyard to be buried.

Della herself nearly died at nine years old after contracting pneumonia. A doctor by the name of Drake rode his horse all the way from Fairfield in order to give her lifesaving medicine. Jim Snead was determined not to lose another daughter and spoon-fed Della large amounts of eggnog until the medicine took effect. She spent two months in bed before recovering, and many people said she was the "sickest person they ever saw that got well."

The family had five more children after Eva passed away: Roy in January 1911, Ruby in October 1912, Raymond in May 1916, and Vernon in June 1918. Della's youngest brother James was born in January of 1921.

The Fork Mountain cabin where the Sneads lived was a large, two-story log structure with a downstairs kitchen/dining room, living area, and a back bedroom where Della's parents slept. The cabin had a front and back porch and a large fireplace in the living area that had to be stoked continuously with wood to heat the house. Even though her daddy kept the home fires burning, Della said it was always cold and drafty in the winter months.

The cabin, which was located on the side of a dirt road, was part of an old slave farm that a man from Amherst

The present barn and corn crib

County by the name of Turner bought and operated with his slaves before the Civil War. It was a large plot of land, and the virgin timber was cut and burned. When the land was cleared, they raised tobacco, wheat, and corn after the war ended. The property was later divided into smaller tracts and sold to local people. Many years ago, the overseer's house was struck by lightning and burned to the ground, but the original cabin, barn, and corn crib still remain.

Some of the family's neighbors out on Fork Mountain were the Bryants, Seamans, Fitzgeralds, and Bradleys. Della's grandparents on her father's side were Walter Downey Snead Sr. (December 20, 1849–June 6, 1900) and Azella Maria Campbell Snead (March 21, 1854–February 24, 1935). A tidbit of information about Della given to me by her family was that she was given her grandmother's first name, Azella, which she never liked. Della was listed on the 1910 and the 1920 census records as Azella Snead, but on the 1930 census her name had changed to "Della." It is not known whether she, in her twenties, officially changed her name or if she just began referring to herself as Della, and that name stuck for the rest of her life.

Della's grandparents on her mother's side were Martin Luther Fitzgerald (June 24, 1854–April 2, 1913) and Mary Elizabeth "Lizzie" Carr Fitzgerald (September 20, 1854–May 5, 1941). Her maternal great-grandparents were Jim Henry Anderson and Mary Elizabeth "Betsy" Fitzgerald Anderson (July 16, 1833–July 7, 1924). Jim Henry was Mary Elizabeth's first husband, who died after the Civil War in November 1865. She later married Achilles Washington Fitzgerald (August 8, 1844–February 5, 1917).

The Fitzgeralds lived in a house that overlooked Crabtree Falls, and Della always found their home to be a real curiosity, being able to watch the water plunge down over the steep rocks right from the house. Both Achilles and Mary Elizabeth are buried at the foot of Crabtree Falls in a small enclosed cemetery. Della was told that Mary Elizabeth was a pretty woman and never had much of this world's goods, but she shared the little she had with her less fortunate neighbors.

Della's father, like so many other men of that era, was a farmer and did his share of logging with a team of horses. In addition to the large vegetable garden needed for the family's food supply, they raised corn, wheat, rye, and buckwheat, which was a real treat when ground and made into pancakes. Jim also had a home apple orchard that was used as a food source as well.

The story is told that Della's father, Jim, was several weeks old, and the family hadn't named him yet. James Crist, a salesman, came through the area selling apple tree starts, and the Sneads bought an orchard packet from him. They liked his name so well that they named their son after him. Jim was born on September 29, 1881, and died on November 27, 1967. His wife, Mary Elizabeth "Betty" Fitzgerald Snead, was born in 1887 and died in 1926. Jim later married his second wife, Lena Butler Perry Snead, who was born in 1905 and died in 1993.

As a tribute to the mountain people's tenacity and endurance, they farmed land so rugged that valley people would never consider tilling it and made it produce a bountiful harvest. Della laughed and said the soil was so rocky it was hard to find enough dirt to hill up the corn. The Sneads also raised hogs that were butchered in the late autumn; they canned the sausage meat and salted the hams and shoulders for later use. They kept milk cows, and Della said she reckoned she had probably churned over a hundred and fifty gallons of butter in her lifetime. The cows had bells attached to their leather collars so the family could tell where they were grazing on the mountainside. Chickens were used for meat and eggs, and the eggs were traded at one of the local country stores when they needed coffee, sugar, or salt.

Della recalls there were several stores in the Montebello area when she was growing up. In the early days, one was operated by a man named John Painter, who later sold his farm and headed west to Idaho. Albert Farris, who was from Syria, was also a storekeeper, along with a man named Seaman. Della remembers walking to the store in Montebello with her brother to get groceries for their mother and carrying them the four miles back home. Those were the days when coffee sold for five cents a pound.

Montebello in the early days

Beauregard "Bewie" Harvey operated a grist mill in Montebello where people took their grain to be ground into flour and meal. Della rode in the wagon with her father many times, accompanying him to the Harvey Mill. The grain was put into large sacks, and when it was ground, it was put back into the same sacks and taken home, where it was emptied into wooden storage barrels.

The Sneads attended Mount Paran Baptist Church, riding in a horse-drawn wagon to Sunday school and morning worship services. One of the circuit-riding preachers who came regularly to Mount Paran was Riley Fitzgerald. Della wore clothing her mother had made, and her long hair was either braided or left loose; it was a pretty dark brown color that she always liked. At twelve years of age, she was baptized and became a member of Mount Paran. At that time, the church homecoming and revival services were held in August, and those wanting to join were baptized in a deep hole in the creek that ran beside Zink's Mill Road, close to the church.

The Snead children attended the one-room schoolhouse on Fork Mountain, which taught grades 1–7. Della walked the mile and a half with her siblings to attend classes. One of her teachers was Effie Payne of Lovingston, who boarded with Pamphlin and Ella Bradley while she taught at the school. In the winter months when it snowed, the Snead children either stayed home or their father would take them to school in a horse-drawn sleigh. Della enjoyed her studies and after finishing her education, went on to teach a few years at the Fork Mountain School before she married. She said that a four-room school was later built in Montebello that included the eighth and ninth grades.

When Della was seventeen, she went to Lynchburg and worked at Randolph Macon College from 1924 to 1925. She worked in the dining hall and said the work was very easy, and she enjoyed it. The next year, her mother took ill, and she didn't go back. Her mother died in July 1926 in UVA Hospital in Charlottesville after doctors mistakenly administered a blood transfusion using the wrong blood type. She died at thirty-nine years of age.

After her mother's death, Della remained at the family home another eighteen months before marrying Robert Fulton Fitzgerald, a young man from Irish Creek whom she had met at Mount Paran Church, where his parents, Dorsey and Eulie Fitzgerald, also attended. Although Fulton was a few years older than Della, she was attracted to him, in her words, "because he came from a good Christian family, and I thought he'd make me a good husband!" When asked if he did, Della smiled and emphatically said, "He sure did . . .

Fulton and Della before marriage

one of the very best!" Fulton's great-grandfather and Della's great-grandmother were brother and sister.

On August 20, 1927, the young couple made the trip to the Lovingston courthouse to be wed. Della's father drove Fulton's father's car (Fulton's father was deceased) and witnessed the ceremony along with Rev. Bob Allen, who was a distant cousin of Fulton. Once married, the couple lived with Fulton's mother for a short time before moving to a house they rented near Mount Paran. Their first two children, Edgar and Edsel, were born in Montebello before the Fitzgeralds moved to Amherst in the Buffalo Creek area and bought a five hundred acre tract of land that Fulton cut timber from and started his own sawmill.

Della said that her husband was a very industrious man and always worked hard and made them a good living. Two more children, Helen and Curtis, were born while they lived at the Amherst home. They made a final move to Willow, at a home they referred to as "The Whitten Place." The last two children, Calvert and Wayne, were born at Willow.

Della said that they were all good children and learned the value of hard work early in life. They have all done well and made their parents proud. Several sons have followed in their father's footsteps and made their life's work in the sawmill and lumber business.

Della said she remains a longtime Democrat, just like her father before her, and has voted in every election since she was old enough to do so. Her only lapse in parties was the time her two sons, Edsel and Calvert, talked her into voting Republican when Richard Nixon was running for president. "It was the worst mistake I ever made," Della retorted strongly, "and right after that, I went back to being a strict Democrat!" Another good laugh the family always shared is the story of Edsel as a child coming in the house and announcing to his mother, "We got two good friends out there, God and Roosevelt!"

Della's beloved husband, Fulton, passed away in January 1982 after a long illness. She continued living at the Willow home after his death for a total of fifty-eight years in all. Years later, she made the move to Buena Vista to be closer to Calvert and his wife, Mary, who live just down the street. She remained close to each of her children and often made the trip across country to her daughter Helen's home in Texas.

As the interview wound down, I asked Della her thoughts about the differences in today's world as opposed to when she grew up.

"I am proud of my family. Fulton and I did our best to raise our children right, and God has been very good to me and blessed me so much. I have had it much better than my parents and the early pioneers who came to this country and settled in a wilderness. Back then, the older people didn't have the things we do now, but they made a good living—had enough to eat and lived good. Things now are very different; we have more material things and have seen more in the world, but people seem to be paying the price by being too busy and not even having enough time to know their neighbors. I have lived in a progressive age. I've seen television and radio, airplanes and numerous other modern inventions, and even watched men walk on the moon. There are parts of my life I'd like to live over again, but, like they say, 'You can't go back.'"

Della passed away in October 2003 at ninety-six years of age, just a few months after I interviewed her, but I will always

Della at ninety-six years of age

treasure meeting and talking with her. I guess you cannot go back in time, but how wonderful it was that she still had memories of an earlier century. A time when a father and his family made mountain music; walked barefoot down a dirt road without a car in sight; and listened to a whippoorwill's haunting evening song, the distant tinkling of cow bells on the hillside, and the laughter of loved ones as they shared a story on the front porch.

Della got to live during a simpler age and had what we all long for in this hurried world of technology: peace of mind, quietness of the heart, and time to savor life to its fullest.

Note: Portions of the above story were taken from Della's writings that were published in the Fitzgerald Family Association's newsletter. Family photos and other information were graciously given by Calvert and Mary Fitzgerald, Marlene Fitzgerald, Betty Haines, and Johnnie Woody.

Restorer Glenn Wilson at his home

14

Glenn Wilson– Log Cabin Restoration

I was really excited when Glenn agreed to be part of *Crazy Quilt*, knowing how he prefers being in the background instead of out front. But after a little urging from his sweet wife, Penny, and some badgering on my part, he relented. I had the privilege of interviewing his mother, LaRue Fauber Wilson, in my book *Appalachian Heart*, and I marveled at how this woman accomplished so much in her life. LaRue was an accomplished musician, farmer, and seamstress, sewing beautiful one-of-a-kind quilts. Her home was filled with intricate handwork, stenciling, and artwork by her own hand. At eighty-four years of age, she was in the process of rechinking the cement in a small log building located on her farm and helping her sons mow the grass and feed the cattle.

So it stands to reason that her son, Glenn, would follow in the family's farming footsteps and find his own area in which to shine. He has a love of all things from earlier centuries, and his profession and his home reflect that connection. I am grateful that there are still people like Glenn who value and respect their ancestors and the special time in history in which they lived. Many, *many* thanks to Glenn Wilson for doing his part to preserve this early culture for generations to come.

The earliest members of the Wilson family lived in Pennsylvania and later moved to Virginia and settled in the Mint Spring area around 1735. They, like so many others who emigrated to the United States, were of Scottish/Irish descent. Within ten years, the Wilsons acquired land in the Steele's Tavern/Raphine area, built homes, and lived on the property. One such home, called the Samuel Wilson house, is a two-story log cabin built in 1791 that was located on a farm on the backside of Steele's Tavern.

The 1791 Samuel Wilson home

Glenn, who has farmed his entire life, was renting that farm in 1978 from a man who wanted to sell him the property. Glenn said, "I had been selling the owner hay, and my grandfather, James Moore Wilson Sr., told me that farm is where all our people came from. The last time he had been over there was in the 1950s, so I took him over there to see it one day. I heard the owner was getting ready to burn the old house and the barn down, so I traded him a couple of hundred bales of hay for the house and the log barn, which was not in good shape. It took me two years to take them down because I was on the road so much shearing." Glenn explained that he sheared sheep all over the state of Virginia into North Carolina and north to Harrisburg, Pennsylvania. He said he was on the road roughly six months out of the year.

When he got ready to move the log house and barn to his present property, one end of the house was gone—taken down in the 1930s—so he went back to the foundation and measured the original size when the whole house sat on it. When he laid out the new foundation, he built it the same size as the original, salvaging logs from the barn to reconstruct the missing end. Glenn explained, "I didn't know where the rooms were in the original house, but my early Sunday school teacher, Mildred Koogler, who was born and raised in the house, did. She and her brothers came over one day while it was under construction and basically showed us where the walls were formerly located."

Glenn finished building his home in 1982. Because the work was visible from the road, a man stopped to ask if Glenn would be interested in working on the man's log cabin when Glenn was finished with his own. That was the start of Glenn's business, Olde Log and Stone, and he has been in the log cabin–reconstruction profession ever since. In addition to taking old log structures down and rebuilding them on other sites, Glenn is a seller of reclaimed materials, such as logs, wood, and stone; he also purchases the same.

He renovates old structures, such as mills, barns, farmhouses, log cabins, and workshops, restoring them to their former glory. He uses natural stone sourced locally to build or rebuild chimneys and fireplaces, foundations, stepping stones, retaining walls, sidewalks, or anything else that stone can be used for. Glenn can do as little or as much of the work as people want. From moving a basic structure and erecting it in a new location to complete turnkey finish work on a log cabin that will be used as a private home.

In 2014, Chad Groah started working with Glenn and quickly became an invaluable partner in the business. Most of the Groah families are based in Vesuvius, and the men are widely known for their carpentry skills, so Chad was well suited for the work he has been called to do.

Cabin at Buffalo Springs Herb Farm

Currently, Glenn and Chad are moving a large log home that was located at the Rockbridge Vineyard in Raphine and erecting it down the road on the former Buffalo Springs Herb Farm property. This is a boon for the men, because it is close to home. Don Haynie and Tom Hamlin, past owners of the farm, made their property a sought-after destination for the local community as well as those living farther away. After the men sold Buffalo Springs, they moved to a cabin Glenn had previously built in Brownsburg.

The farthest points from which Glenn has moved cabins are Dalton, Georgia, and Killington, Vermont. He esti-

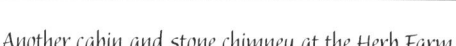

Another cabin and stone chimney at the Herb Farm

mates that he has moved well over one hundred buildings. Glenn also restored a log cabin (the McGuffey house) at the Henry Ford Museum in Dearborn, Michigan. Glenn

The Haynie/Hamlin cabin in Brownsburg

Penny and Glenn Wilson

said log buildings in Virginia are getting harder and harder to find, although he now has equipment in Brookneal that is taking down four tobacco barns. He finds a lot of usable log structures in North Carolina, as well as some in Tennessee.

Glenn and his wife, Penny, married in 2007, and she not only supports his work but also goes with him to festivals and helps with some of his building designs. They met when she was working at the Buffalo Springs Herb Farm while Glenn was coming in and out, building several of the log structures there. Penny is a very talented woman in her own right. She is a broom maker, she hooks rugs, sews, makes soap, farms, and tends the family's vegetable garden. She is also a Master Gardener as well as a member of the Herb Guild, and she does a lot of volunteer work.

She is a collector of rye baskets (baskets woven from rye straw), and between the two of them, their collection has bloomed to 160 baskets. This type of basket was utilitarian and was used for all types of storage. Penny also has a pen-

Penny's broom shop

chant for early bee skeps made out of rye straw, and their rustic home has quite a few on display.

October is their busiest month, and the day we talked, they were getting ready to participate in an Expo that weekend, making apple butter the following week, and then on to Hickory, North Carolina, for another festival near the end of the month.

The Wilsons lease three farms close to their home and raise a cross of Angus/Limousine cattle and Boer

Interior of the broom shop

The cozy interior of the Wilson cabin

goats that are used for meat. Goat meat has become the fastest growing meat in the last twenty years, and Glenn keeps about forty nanny goats at present. Glenn said his paternal grandparents (James Moore Sr. and Blanche Wilson), his parents (James Moore Jr. and LaRue Wilson), and his maternal grandparents (Hercy and Lottie Fauber) always kept sheep, as did many of the people in and around Montebello. Glenn raised sheep until the market took a nose dive. He sold his flocks along with the herding dogs. In the spring of 1996, a nail punctured his left eye, and the doctors told him not to bend over. That's when he completely gave up sheep shearing for good. But farming is in his blood, a family tradition that is an intrinsic part of who Glenn Wilson is.

Glenn is a wealth of information concerning early log structures, and I learned a lot by just listening to him. For instance, the word "chinking." Most people think that chinking is the cement that's put in between the logs. Glenn explained that true chinking is just something that takes up the space between the logs. Many times, slabs of wood were used, cut to fit and laid at an angle between each log. We found these smooth pieces of wood laid diagonally between the logs of Billy's cabin homeplace after the cement had cracked and fallen out.

Two cabins with a middle dogtrot (a covered walkway between two separate structures)

The cement part is called "daubing," and, in earlier times, it consisted of creek sand, lime, and clay with hog or horse hair mixed in. Today, Glenn sprays foam insulation between the logs, then fits galvanized lath screen on each side of the foam, and finishes daubing the screen with mortar. This method gives added insulation to a log cabin home, making it warmer in the winter and cooler in the summer. He will also tint the mortar according to the soil type in the area where the cabin will be located.

Glenn explained another misconception that people have about log cabins. "Most people think old logs in cabins are all made of chestnut. There are chestnut cabins where there were chestnut trees growing. But people didn't go ten miles down the road to get a chestnut log. They used whatever type of wood was growing where they owned land and where they were clearing. If the land was supported by mostly hardwood, then that is what they built their cabins from. But there are plenty of poplar logs in cabins, too. My own home has a few chestnut logs, but black walnut, poplar, and cherry as well. Of all the buildings I've ever seen, there is only one that was made entirely of chestnut; the logs, floor joists, rafters, flooring, and sheeting boards were all of chestnut. That house came from House Mountain."

I asked what the oldest cabin he's ever taken down was, and Glenn said it was probably his own house, which was built in 1791. The newest building was a tobacco barn that was hewn out in 1938, which Glenn took down and put back up for a neighbor's guest house.

A neighbor's tobacco barn guest house

The average time it takes Glenn to take a building down and produce a turnkey home, move-in ready, is dependent on the size of the building. A good estimate would be six months to a year. He uses a combination of vintage hand tools and more modern tools and equipment for his restoration work.

The biggest building he has ever undertaken was the old Wiseman house in Greenville, Virginia. It is a pair of two-story log houses joined together; they took Glenn eighteen months to disassemble and move to Timber Ridge. He is also responsible for all the log buildings at the Cyrus McCormick Farm in Raphine and maintains the large waterwheel at the mill.

At the Cyrus McCormick Mill

I asked if he ever would consider building a new cabin, and Glenn emphatically said, "No!" The reason? He feels that today's wood will not hold up like the old logs. "The quality of the wood . . . the size of the wood is not here anymore. The good wood is all going for export. If I could get a load of good clear hemlock or hemlock that wasn't dead over a year, then I might consider it. Anything dead over a year, the sap has gone out of it and the bugs have pretty much destroyed the tree. People don't realize it, but hemlock is the most moisture and bug resistant wood that we have here in the valley, but the wooly adelgid insect has destroyed a lot of them."

A dry-stacked chimney

When asked what the worst part of the job is, Glenn said that it's the unavailability of good materials, plus the lack of people he can find that do this kind of work. But he is quick to praise the men he can count on in a pinch. He said that the Bradley brothers out of Stuarts Draft, who do framing work, have been lifesavers for him over the years. And when Glenn finally decides to retire, he is hoping that Chad will succeed him in the business.

Glenn said that the absolute best part is that he loves every facet of what he does. He enjoys taking down log buildings and reconstructing them. And he loves the stonework involved in building chimneys and fireplaces. "I could lay stone all day long," he said.

I commented on the stone wall and outdoor patio he had built for his neighbor, asking what the small semicircular concrete object was in the middle of the wall. The object in question is a wood-fired oven that can be used for baking bread, pizza, and the like, which is a pretty neat addition to anyone's patio.

As the interview wound down, I asked Glenn how he had learned to do his particular trade. Did someone teach him, or was it just raw talent that was always inside him? He wisely related, "We all have hidden talents, but nowadays people don't know what their talent is, what they are actually capable of."

Doctor Robert Hart, a family physician in Hickory, North Carolina, has rescued and restored a collection of artifacts and buildings of nineteenth-century Carolina life, creating an entire village in Catawba County. It is the largest private collection of original, historical log structures in the United States. On the cover of a book about Dr. Hart, a quote caught my eye: "One man's passionate preservation of North Carolina's pioneer heritage."

And, basically, I believe that quote also applies to Glenn Wilson. He is a man passionate about his restoration work and doing his best to preserve and pass on the heritage of an earlier time in history.

Anyone wishing more information about Glenn's restoration work may contact him through his Facebook page at Olde Log and Stone or call him at 540-377-5939.

One of Glenn's wood-fired bread ovens

View of the Tye River Valley from 20 Minute Cliff

15

"It's More Than a Wilderness"

"Hey, Dad, what's down there?"
"Nothing, son, it's just a big wilderness."
I was sitting on a rock ledge below the retaining wall, hidden from the eyes of the father and son who were discussing the view from 20 Minute Cliff at milepost 19 on the Blue Ridge Parkway. Just three miles from my home at Love, this is the place I come to when I want a bit of peace. Many's the time I've packed an early breakfast and eaten it out on the rocks, watching the golden sun come up over the shadowed ridges, then have driven back later in the evening to enjoy hot coffee from a thermos, watching the same red sun slowly sink behind the darkening mountains.

I never tire of looking down at the deep crevice separating Fork Mountain and Dowell's Ridge, which runs from Montebello through the Tye River Valley below. It was the home of so many people I've known and heard about since moving here in 1980.

That's why I found the conversation between the boy and his father so amusing. Unknowingly, all the father saw was an uninhabited, endless wilderness of trees. Looking down the steep cleft, my eyes saw an entirely different picture—one heaped with memories.

The first time I realized the view I enjoyed from the cliff was vastly different from what it used to be was the time I took my neighbor, Johnny Coffey, then in his nineties, for a ride to the overlook. Johnny, with a sweeping motion of his hand, said the one sentence that has never ceased to amaze me: "Son, it's hard to believe that seventy-five years ago, you could look out and see no trees on those mountains."

What was he talking about? As far as the eye could see, every ridge was covered in a dense forest. Thinking I hadn't heard him correctly, I asked for more details.

"Why, son, when I was a young boy, the mountains here were covered with Kentucky bluegrass . . . grazing land for people's cattle and sheep. There were a few hammocks of trees here and there for shade for the animals, but for the most part it was all open land, and you could see folks' homeplaces along Fork Mountain and down below at White Rock."

I instinctively glanced downward at the white house far below, the one belonging to Hercy and Burgess Coffey. It was now the only visible house you could see from the cliff. It was said that the overlook got its name from the people of White Rock who used it as a timepiece, knowing that when the evening sun hit the rock face, they had exactly twenty minutes before dusk would fall. Twenty minutes in which to shut the door to the hen house and herd the cows and sheep into the safety of the barn for the night.

In addition to the Coffeys, families by the names of Fitzgerald, Allen, Taylor, Campbell, and Carr lived on these steep ridges, carving out a self-sufficient living from the rocky land.

What a treasure-house of memories I have: driving up the North Fork of the Tye River, visiting Preacher Billy Morris, who lived in the old Mitchell Fitzgerald home; attending family reunions at Raymond and Maggie Allen's remote camp on Durham's Run; and watching Annie Ramsey making floured biscuits on her wood cookstove. And many were the times I made the trip over to White Rock the night before trout season opened to listen to old-time mountain music being played at the different camps.

Annie Carr had a perfect view of Squaremouth Rocks from the porch of her home. The rocks are located on a steep cliff at the end of Chicken Holler and have a square opening leading into a small cave. This cave is thought to have been inhabited by Native Americans before the Scottish/Irish people began settling the mountainous area.

Johnny would make the old-time church revivals come alive in my mind as he'd tell of people walking to the "night meetings" with lanterns in hand. "Why there were so many folks walking to church back then that the mountains glittered like lightening bugs."

Time has a way of changing everything. One generation's memories are never the same as the one before. And seventy-five years can make an amazing difference between one man seeing a "wilderness" and another one seeing "home."

The present Oak Hill Baptist Church

16

Oak Hill Baptist Church, Massies Mill

I have long admired the beautiful white church sitting high atop a hill with the big DePriest mountain as a backdrop. The sign for the church at the junction of Dickie Road and Level Green had always fascinated me because of the early date—1869—just a few years after the Civil War had ended. I was a vendor at the old Fleetwood School at one of the spring trail rides and was seated next to a kind lady by the name of Sandra Vaughn. I learned her family attended Oak Hill Church, and when I asked if the pastor would be interested in letting me write the history of the old church for *Crazy Quilt*, she gave me his name and phone number.

I called Rev. Edward Hendricks; he said yes; and the result was a delightful afternoon at the church with Pastor Hendricks; deacons Joseph Gaines, Calvin Green, and Delores Green; and church secretary, Veronica Glover. All were so kind to open the doors of Oak Hill as well as their hearts.

The membership of the church is very gifted in many areas, and their desire is to serve God and the community in any way he leads. The church will celebrate its 150th anniversary in 2019, and I pray it will continue to be a beacon of God's light in our world, and he will bless it for many more years to come.

Oak Hill Baptist Church was organized in the nineteenth century at Jonesboro Baptist church. In 1860, Jonesboro enrolled 182 negro members. Six years later, in 1866, the membership had increased to 250. Because of that growth, the black members united and came together as a church body but continued to worship at Jonesboro until 1869, when they moved and built their own temple to worship God, calling themselves Oak Hill Baptist Church.

The name "Oak Hill" was derived from the location in which the church was built—an area on a hill surrounded by beautiful oak trees. The church was built of hewn logs, which was not an uncommon building material in those days. Rev. Alexander Giles was the first pastor. Other members of the official board were deacons Lemmon Meade, James Smith, Jacob Napier, Boyd Loving, Mosely Gaines, Roland Johnson, Alexander Hughes, and Joe Henley. The church custodians were Jashie Robertson and Ned Smith.

After twelve years of service in the little log sanctuary, a frame church was built from lumber brought from an area called Shelter Bottom. Jackson Loving and his sister, Jane Johnson, transported this lumber to the building site by the use

Early church drawing by Liz Bryant

of a two-wheel cart pulled by a team of oxen that belonged to Boyd Loving.

In 1883, the "Rockfish Baptist Association" met at Oak Hill Church under the leadership of Revs. Rubin Loving and Richard Hughes.

In the early 1900s, Oak Hill School was established on the church grounds. Originally, the two-room building housed children from the primer level through the eighth grade. The school benefited under the tutelage of many instructors, but its most profound impact to the community came under the leadership of Othello R. Wilson. Through his expertise in music, he opened up a new world for the students by organizing the Musical Arts Choir that included students aged six to sixteen. This group was, at times, called the Sunday school choir, as they shared their voices in the services of the church.

The choir traveled to many places in concert. Among the schools toured were Hampton Institute, Virginia State College, Sweet Briar College, Roanoke College, William and Mary, Randolph Macon College, Southern College, and

The Oak Hill School

Hollins College. These tours generated monetary gifts that were used to purchase school supplies and establish two additional rooms. At that time, several grades above the eighth grade were added.

After the former Nelson Training High School for Blacks was opened in 1941, the Oak Hill School reverted to the elementary level grades. In 1952, it closed after the modern Massies Mill Elementary School was built.

In earlier years, baseball was a favorite pastime for many Nelson County citizens. Before Jackie Robinson bridged the discrimination gap in 1947, there were blacks with superior skills who played in rough, open fields. Fulton Ligon, a black entrepreneur, organized a team in Massies Mill in the 1920s and 1930s and was instrumental in supporting its success by contacting other sandlot teams to play against. His team traveled in trucks throughout the state of Virginia, and later, by bus, they ventured to West Virginia, Maryland, and Washington, DC, to play.

Home games were played in an enclosed field in Massies Mill and were enjoyed by all who could pay the admission charge. Team members committed to the task were Robert Giles, Thomas Ligon, Alex Giles, Hiawatha Giles, Garfield Giles, Otis Ligon, Tom Giles, William Epps, Johnny Steptoe, Alphonso Ligon, Phil Toliver, Edward Giles, Ben Vaughan, and the all-time great pitcher, Buster Giles. Buster tried out with the Homestead Grays but, because his family didn't want him to leave, he returned home.

Fulton Ligon was an industrious and successful business man and a professional carpenter who built the Oak Hill Church and was also responsible for a bus to transport the children to and from school. He owned a store, a lumber business, a funeral home, and houses in the Massies Mill area. He saw the need for community involvement, so constructed a social hall that was used for various meetings, a night school, and dances.

By 1900, Oak Hill's membership had increased tremendously, thereby motivating them to build a larger church in 1923 under the leadership of Rev. William Bailey, the second minister of Oak Hill. The new church was built by Fulton Ligon. The church clerk, officers, deacons, and trustees were all established at this time. The church clerk was Addison Brown. Other officers of the church were deacons George Witts, Peter Page, Pleasant Wood, Paul Jones, Edward Allen, Phillip Napier, and Jacob Johnson. Deacons of the younger generation were Bland Thompson, Otis Ligon, Mathew Gaines, Walton Vaughan, George and Dandridge Oakcrum, Drew Allen, James Walter Thompson, Johnnie Jackson, and Leonard Brown. Trustees were Patrick Epps, William Henry Thompson, William Johnson, Rubin Vaughan, Ralph Meade, Thomas Thompson, William Mason, and Alexander Meade.

Beginning in 1941, Rev. Herman Goode served as the church's third pastor. He was followed by Rev. Thomas M.

The growing congregation at Oak Hill

McClendon, who served the congregation for ten years. During his leadership, several clubs were started, and donations were raised for the stained-glass windows, a walkway, and hymnals for the church.

Rev. John W. Pride was installed as Oak Hill's fifth pastor for a short term, and in 1958, a ladies room and choir loft was built by Thomas Ligon. Rev. Reginald A. Johnson became the sixth pastor, and Rev. Alice Coles served as assistant pastor in 1964. The deaconess board was organized, and the membership increased to 420 members.

On March 22, 1970, Rev. Carter R. Wicks Jr. was installed as the seventh pastor of Oak Hill. Under Pastor Wicks's teaching, the church began to have a worship service every Sunday, except the fifth Sunday in a month. Communion was served on the second Sunday of each month, effective January 1971. The following ministers were licensed to preach under Pastor Wicks's administration: Rev. Mae Oakcrum, March 19, 1976; Rev. Joseph Vaughan, October 15, 1978; Rev. Margaret Bowling, November 5, 1978; Rev. Matthews Toms Sr., October 6, 1985; Rev. Edward Gaines, October 9, 1989; Rev. Emma T. Jackson, November 18, 1990; and Rev. Emma Vaughan, December 9, 1990.

The following clubs and/or groups were organized under Pastor Wicks's leadership: the Concerned Club, the Young Adult Fellowship Club, the Building Fund, the Kitchen Committee, the Missionary Circle, the Teenagers Rap Session Club, the Junior Choir, the Toms Sisters, the Toms Family Gospel Chorus, the Willing Workers (also known as the Women's Auxiliary), and the Bailey Memorial Usher Board. The Othello R. Wilson Scholarship Fund was formed in his memory to honor the profound impact he had on area students by helping those seeking higher education.

In June 1970, the Concerned Members of Oak Hill was formed and organized in Washington, DC, by Adrienne Gaines Jordon. This club is a union of outstanding Oak Hill members away from home and noted for its provision of financial aid to improve the facilities of the church. The idea of organizing the club was conceived after the devastating flood of 1969 that claimed the lives of many relatives and friends. Under the leadership of Pastor Wicks, Oak Hill had various improvements, ordinations, appointments to positions, donations, and purchases—all for the betterment of the church. This included the beautification and renaming of the Oak Hill Cemetery to the Oak Hill Memorial Gardens.

On May 6, 1995, Pastor Wicks retired after more than twenty-five years of service. Rev. Wayne Jackson became the eighth pastor in June 1995. The Oak Hill Mass Choir was organized on August 12, 1995, by Sister Clarissa Jackson and directed by Sister Regina Toms. The Food Pantry was established in 1995 by Deaconess Lecie Barnett. Under her leadership, this food ministry served not only Oak Hill members but also families in the surrounding communities and counties. Pastor Jackson resigned in September 1996. From

The Memorial Garden monument

October 1996 to July 1998, Oak Hill was without a pastor, but various donations and renovations were done to beautify the church. On July 12, 1998, Pastor Lorenzo Keith Otey was installed as the ninth pastor.

During the years of Rev. Otey, Oak Hill ordained ministers John Allen, Lucy Barnett, Ruth Toms-Canada, Annette Diggs, Paula Gaines, and Belle Thomas, to name a few. The bylaws were completed and adopted. A new addition was added that included the kitchen/dining room and fellowship hall, classrooms and conference room, pastor's study, and church office. The parking lot was expanded and paved also.

In 2005, the Kate V. Loving Memorial Scholarship was established by Rachel Loving Hicks to honor the ninetieth birthday of her mother, Kate Viola Loving, a lifelong member of Oak Hill. The mission of the scholarship is to provide funds to high school graduates who are active members of Oak Hill and have been accepted to college with a grade point average of 2.0 or above.

On August 24, 2008, the Oak Hill Memorial Library/Museum opened, which contains artifacts and memorabilia collected to showcase the rich history of Oak Hill. This effort was spearheaded by Deacon Bobby Cabbell.

Pastor Otey resigned in June 2012. Oak Hill prayed faithfully for God to bless them with a new shepherd. God answered their prayers, and on September 15, 2013, he blessed the church with its tenth pastor, Rev. Edward M. Hendricks Jr. On September 16, 2018, the Oak Hill congregation celebrated five years of leadership under Rev. Hendricks.

Rev. Hendricks was raised in the Puppy Creek area of Amherst County. When he was a child, his brother played baseball at Fleetwood, Roseland, and at the Ebony and Ivory Field, and Edward would tag along to watch the games. "As a child, I met all these people from the area, never realizing that much later in life I would become the pastor of Oak Hill and have a relationship with them."

He said that the only two times he had any connection with Oak Hill was when he and a friend were working in Waynesboro and went across the mountain on the way home. "It was revival time, and my friend Keith Thomas had to play the drums for the service, so we stopped; and while he played, I sat quietly in the back of the church. It went so well that we stopped again the next night."

Rev. Edward Hendricks

Edward said that he was in his early thirties at the time and was deeply involved in various ministries at his own church, Scott Zion Baptist Church in Madison Heights. He had never desired to pastor a church, so when the lord began laying that ministry on his heart, Edward started running from what God wanted him to do.

He recalled, "I remember it was a Thursday night, and I started driving east on I-64, crying out to God, telling him I could not carry the mantle according to the way I thought it should be carried. I was about halfway to Richmond when I turned around and drove to my pastor Gary Lee's house about 11:15 that night. When he opened the door, he said 'I knew you would be coming. There had been a tugging on my heart, and God told me somebody would come.'"

Edward wanted to be obedient to God's call but was still somewhat resistant to sending out a resumé to area churches. In 2008, he started getting calls from different congregations, asking if he could come and preach. By 2009, he had married his wife, Amanda, and together they were serving God in different capacities at Scott Zion. He filled the pulpit for several years at different churches before becoming a full-time candidate for two of them. During that time, Oak Hill also wanted him to come and preach as a possible candidate but with one difference—the nine-panel membership wanted to interview him before he came. After the interview, Edward said that he left feeling nervous but later got a call saying they wanted him to come and preach every Sunday for a month, which he did.

"In July of 2013, our family was on vacation at the beach, and on the way to my wife's favorite seafood restaurant (Capt. George's), I got the call from the chairman of the deacon ministry, Joseph Gaines, who said, 'After the votes were counted, the congregation has elected you to be the pastor if you so choose to take the office.' I humbly accepted and began my pastorship at Oak Hill on September fifteenth of that year."

He credits Joseph Gaines for taking him under his wing and introducing him to all the back roads of Nelson County, where many of the Oak Hill members lived.

Rev. Hendricks is going into his sixth year as Oak Hill Baptist Church's pastor and listening to him and other members of the congregation talk, it has been a good fit for all of them. He is currently enrolled at Liberty University in Lynchburg, studying for his BA degree. Edward Hendricks is a humble man of God, seeking only to serve the members of his church and local community. He adds, "I don't ever question my call, but I question my ability from time to time." He speaks freely about the people he shepherds, saying how blessed they are with talent that they use for God's glory.

Throughout the years, Oak Hill has been a vital part of the Nelson County community. They have had a very successful food pantry program, providing food for about seventy families each month. In October 2018, they moved the pantry to the Nelson Heritage Center on Route 29, where the Blue Ridge Area Food Bank has a mobile food pantry. Rev. Hendricks said, "I feel the move is going to greatly impact the area and move from seventy families we are currently serving to between two hundred and three hundred families."

The church has added a computer room, as well as a first aid room in case of emergencies. They still have the extensive history museum in the basement, chronicling Oak Hill's rich history of the past while faithfully documenting present additions in the form of notes, photos, programs, awards, and rewards from the Spirit above.

Rev. Hendricks and his wife, Amanda

A section of the Oak Hill's history museum

(L-R) Deacon Joseph Gaines, secretary Veronica Glover,
Rev. Hendricks, deacons Delores and Calvin Green

There are six different choirs within the church body: the Gospel Chorus, the Mass Choir, Senior Choir, Men's Chorus, the Praise Team, and Youth Choir. They are also blessed with members who are talented musicians who play during services. There is a woman's ministry, an usher's ministry, and the fourth Sunday in August is always reserved as Homecoming Sunday.

The church also developed a community garden, and the harvest was given to anyone who wanted to come and pick fresh vegetables, plus vegetables were taken to seniors and shut-ins. Rev. Hendricks said it was developed on the "3-P" principal: planters, pickers, and providers. I suggested they add a "W" to the mix—weeders! For a future garden, they hope to secure land closer to the church on which to plant and perhaps build a greenhouse.

In October 2019, Oak Hill Baptist Church will be celebrating its 150th anniversary, commemorating its rich history and service to the Nelson County area. Its motto continues to be relevant in today's world: "The Church Where Everybody Is Somebody."

Oak Hill Baptist Church: "The Church Where Everybody Is Somebody"

An old-fashioned Christmas still life

17

Christmas Traditions in the Blue Ridge Mountains

The soft glow of an oil lamp and pine boughs on a windowsill evoke fond memories of an era when Christmas was less commercial and more a time for families to get together and give loved ones simple, handmade gifts from the heart. A tree was brought home from the woods and decorated with garlands of strung popcorn and colorful paper chains. It was a slower time when people had the pleasure of quietly talking around the fire and perhaps peeling some coveted holiday oranges for the little ones. These and many other traditions have been passed down from generation to generation, making Christmas a very special time of year.

Upon moving to the hamlet of Love in 1980, I was determined to make our first Christmas memorable by keeping some of these early traditions alive. Living in a rustic hunting camp building with a high ceiling, I wanted a tall tree to fill one corner of the living room. My neighbor, Gladys Coffey, said that they had some large trees on their property, and I was welcome to cut the top out of one. I shinnied up the trunk of a real beauty, wielding a handsaw, and held on for dear life as the cut portion tumbled to the ground. The tree was so massive it had to be cut several more times before we could get it in the house.

A large tree at the camp

Once in place, it was decorated with red plaid bows, candy canes, pine cones, bird nests, strings of popcorn, and white doves cut out from a box of Christmas cards and placed among the branches. We trooped up the mountain in search of running cedar for the mantle, and mistletoe (which was shot out of oak trees) was hung from a doorway in hopes of a holiday kiss. By the world's standards, the decorations in the camp were plain, but I was thrilled to be carrying on some of the customs that my older neighbors had celebrated when they were growing up.

Hazel Campbell Fitzgerald, who grew up on Hat Creek, relayed this story to me about what her family did at Christmas.

"At Christmastime, we'd put up a tree, and us kids would glue paper chains together to decorate it. Sometimes we'd take the silver paper inside cigarette packs and wrap it around sycamore balls and hang them on the tree, too. Mama and Daddy would go down to Tommy Carter's store and buy each of us kids a little toy of some kind. Us girls usually got a baby doll, but I remember once I got a little wind-up tin toy where a dog chased a cat and the cat chased a fish. I don't know whatever happened to that toy, but I wish I would have hung on to it."

Sending Christmas cards was a popular tradition in earlier years, just as it is today. Many were embossed with beautiful scenes on the front, and a one-cent postage stamp was all it took to send it on its way. I found several of these cards and the stamped envelopes they came in among my late mother-in-law's possessions.

I asked my elderly neighbor, Johnny Coffey, if his family did anything special when he was a child. He said that his mother always baked an apple butter cake for the holiday, and it was something he always looked forward to. Johnny said it was a four-layer pound cake made from scratch with apple butter spread between layers and on top. That Christmas, I attempted to recreate his mother's cake. When it was done, I walked up through the woods to Johnny's house and presented it to him. When he opened the box and saw it, he began to weep and said it was the first one he'd had since his mother died. It was the best gift I ever gave someone—a treasured memory from childhood.

Johnny's apple butter cake

My husband Billy said that Christmas in the holler where he was born was not about getting presents on the morning of December 25th. The holiday stretched out several weeks and consisted of walking to each of his aunts and uncles' homes for a meal and having them, in turn, come back for a meal at their cabin. He said fresh oranges and peppermint sticks were delicious treats he only got during the season, and he recalled receiving very few toys, usually given by one of the relatives. He still has the little horse-drawn metal pull toy given to him by an older cousin.

Entertainments were also popular in the one-room schoolhouses in the Love area. My father-in-law, Saylor, remembered a funny incident that happened at the old Ivy Hill School where the children from the holler attended.

"My older brother, Pettit, came to the program dressed as Santa Claus and was trying to read his part in the play. It was getting dark, so he told me to hold the oil lamp a little

Billy Coffey's metal Christmas toy

closer, so he could read better. When I put the light up to him, I accidentally caught his beard on fire! He ran behind the sheet we had strung across the front of the classroom and put out the fire in his beard so the little children wouldn't

The old Ivy Hill School in the holler

see. Everyone had a big laugh over it. Later in the evening, several people played string music, and everyone enjoyed it."

Lillie Puckett Napier was ninety-four years of age when I interviewed her, and she said Christmas at the Puckett home was one big get-together with neighbors visiting up and down Stoney Creek.

"We would go from house to house, playing games, making candy, sharing a meal. Our family had a live tree that we would decorate. Mama left us kids at Granny's house while she went Christmas shopping in Nellysford.

Lillie Puckett Napier

She told me not to peek inside the bags she brought home, but I did and found two doll babies, one dressed in pink and the other in blue. On Christmas Eve, I told Mama, as I was going upstairs to bed, that I hoped Santa Claus would bring me the dolly in the pink dress. She knew at once I had peeked at the presents!"

Vera Falls, one of nine children, grew up along the North Fork of the Tye River and told me that Christmas was a time her mother did a lot of baking.

"She would bake cakes, pies, and donuts for us. We'd cut a tree and decorate it with anything we could make and hang candy canes on it. In the fall, we all got a new pair of shoes that we were so proud of, and we would save the shoe boxes and put them on top of the table for Santa Claus to fill. On Christmas morning, the boxes would have oranges, nuts, and candy in them—things we didn't get every day."

Vera Coffey Falls

For people who were born in the late nineteenth and early twentieth centuries, these simple traditions were part of their lives and will never be forgotten. But modern-day people have started traditions all their own, making unforgettable memories equally important to their children and grandchildren.

Brian and Kristin Gembara, who live near Chicago but have family roots in Nelson County, Virginia, started a tradition of opening gifts on Christmas Eve and giving matching pajamas to their two children. As the children became teenagers, Kris thought they may find the matching pajamas babyish, so she and Brian joined in and began wearing them, too, continuing a fun family tradition. On Christmas night, after all the family visiting is over, they go to a late movie.

Chris and Penny Miller and their two sons always go out to eat at a Chinese restaurant on Christmas Eve; in the morning, they go to Penny's mother's house for a Christmas breakfast and back again later for a big meal with friends and the rest of the family.

Stacy Johnson of Afton, her husband, Todd, and their three daughters have a tradition of having the family in on Christmas Eve and serving the same exact snacks and finger foods each year. Later in the evening, they all sit down to watch Earl Hamner's classic, *The Homecoming: A Christmas Story*. Stacy also puts up and decorates multiple trees throughout her home.

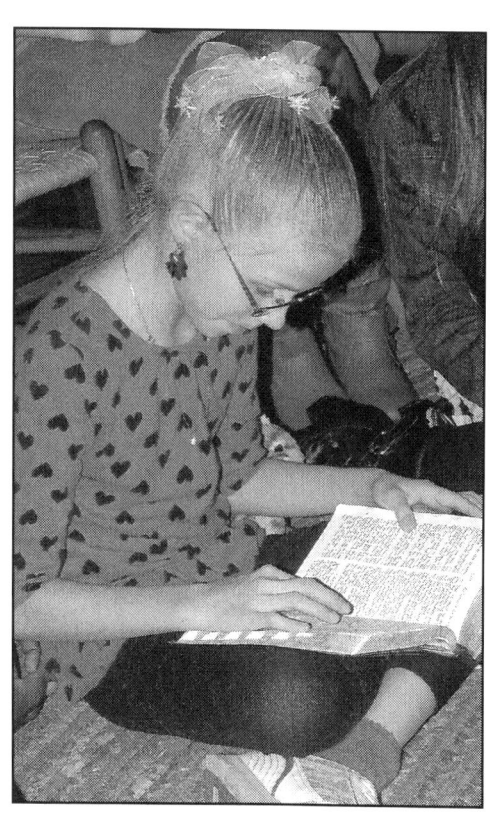

Tressia Coffey reading the Christmas story

In our own home, before we begin opening presents, we have a tradition of letting one of our grandchildren read the Christmas story from the second chapter of Luke's gospel, reminding us again that the greatest gift to mankind is God's son.

Ethel Allen Matheny at ninety-six years of age

18

The Journal
The Childhood Memories of Lora Ethel Fitzgerald Allen Matheny

Note: In twenty-five years of publishing *Backroads* newspaper, Ethel was often included in interviews, family reunions, and photographs. When I shared with Gary Allen that I was going to write another book, he asked if I would be interested in his Grandmother Ethel's handwritten journal about her early childhood memories. Reading it is such a treasure, and I'm glad she had the foresight to pen her experiences on paper. Thanks to Gary for bringing it to light and not letting her written words molder, forgotten in an attic. Although there is no date as to when Ethel wrote this journal, she was born in 1903 and died in 2005 at 102 years of age.

My memory started as a child back [when I was] very young, while Aunt Susan Wood was still living. Also her sickness and death from blood poisoning when a chestnut burr pricked her hand. Papa bathed her hand in carbolic acid and dressed it daily. I remember her funeral. Papa held me up in his arms, and I had on black patent slippers. It's funny to remember what I wore, being so young.

I was the fourth child born to my parents, Alfred McElroy Fitzgerald (Jan. 8, 1879–May 9, 1966) and Lelia Burgess Bradley Fitzgerald (May 14, 1879–Oct. 16, 1918). I was born on May 4, 1903.

The Alfred Fitzgerald family; Ethel is standing to her father's left

We lived at what we called the "Old Place" at that time. It contained 43 acres of land. Next, I can remember when my sister Velma was born. My older sister Pearlie took us smaller

Foundation stones at the old homeplace

children, and we went to Grandma Sophia and Grandpa Henry's. We had to leave home before breakfast and walk the short distance. Pearlie took eggs for us to eat for breakfast in a half-gallon molasses bucket. When we returned home, a little black-haired baby was lying in bed with Mama, and that was Velma. After she was born, Grandpa Henry, who was a Baptist preacher, decided we needed a larger house to live in, so Papa and our family moved over to where they lived, and they moved over to where we lived. I remember us moving, and the first night we were staying in our new house I had to sleep upstairs. I was five years old, and Papa sat by my bed until I went to sleep because I was afraid. It was too early for Pearlie to come to bed, because they all had work to do after moving in.

Grandpa Henry decided to sell Papa the house we had just moved in for five hundred dollars if he would take care of him and Grandma Sophia for the rest of their life. Papa did take care of them, and later they moved in with us, and we loved having them there. When they lived to themselves, I had to carry a half-gallon of fresh milk daily to them and keep them in eggs, pork meat, and vegetables. Sometimes Pearlie had to go with me if we had much to carry to them.

Our grandparents never scolded us at any time. They were always so kind and good to us. When they lived alone, we would go see them, and they always had pound cake or wheat bread baked in what we call hoe cake. They would give us a slice of cake or split the piece of bread and put butter and jam or some other kind of preserves between the bread. We really did like that it was so tasty.

I had two sisters and one brother older than me. I was the fourth born in our family. There were seven children in all: Lottie Burgess, Lula Pearl, William Boyd, Lora Ethel, Henry Claiborne, Ollie Velma, and Dura Mabel. We grew up on a farm in Nelson County, Virginia, and there was always work to do on a farm. The older ones had to work in the fields,

Ethel on left with sisters Mabel and Velma

getting up hay, hoeing corn, and feeding cattle, sheep, and hogs. My job was carrying water to the field in a small bucket for them to drink and milking cows during the summer. Claiborne and myself did most of the milking during the summer, and we had a big yellow cat that learned to follow us to the milking gap, as we called it, and we would squirt milk in his mouth every day until he'd be full.

Claiborne and I usually worked together, and we walked to Montebello to get the mail and a few groceries. As soon as we were old enough, we would carry a few eggs and sometimes an old hen to sell to pay for what we bought. Mama kept chickens, a few turkeys, ducks, geese, and some guineas. The guineas would hide their nests of eggs, and we'd have a terrible time trying to find them. When the ducks and geese would make a nest of their own, they would begin laying their eggs, and you had to take a large spoon to get their eggs out from under them. If you put your hand in the nest, they would move and make a new one, and then you would have to hunt forever to find their new nest.

The Childhood Memories of Lora Ethel Fitzgerald Allen Matheny

Growing up on a farm meant that everyone had a work chore. We grew up in a Christian home where we always went to church on Sunday. Mama and Papa got up early, and he and William went to the barn to feed the stock and then came back to the house where my mother would have a big breakfast cooked. Before we ate, we all went to the living room where Papa read the Bible and said a prayer.

Going to school was a must, and as soon as we were old enough, we would go. If the weather was too bad for us to walk, Papa always took us horseback; or if it was a deep snow, he would hook up his farm sled and take us. He would also pick up other children on the way if they wanted a ride. We only had seven months of school at that time. I finished the seventh grade and we had no high school near us.

Early Fork Mountain School and children

Lottie got married to Harper Steele when she was only fifteen years old. Papa sold him twenty-nine acres of land, and Harper built a house close to us, and it is still standing there. Grandpa Henry married them on an August Sunday

Fork Mountain School today

at the beginning of what they called the "Big Meeting," now called a revival. It lasted each day through Friday. There was a service at eleven o'clock and dinner on the grounds and another service at two o'clock. Papa always had a farm wagon, so he would hook up two horses and take the family each day to church. Mama had to cook for each day's lunch at church. William and I got old enough to walk with neighbor friends. Saturday was the baptizing day at the mill dam in old Montebello. We had lots of fun walking, but when I got too old (thirteen), I began to date. Since it was Perry Allen, Uncle Davis Allen's son, Papa didn't say anything to me. He had told me I could not date young, but since Pearlie had also married at age fifteen to Talmage Campbell, he let me be. They got married on March 15, 1914.

At this time, Grandpa Henry and Grandma Sophia were still living with us and after Talmage and Pearl were married, they went to live in Papa's house, which we called the "Old Place." My grandparents went to live with them, and Grandpa had a stroke that July. A blood vessel broke in his head while he was sitting on the porch, and he fell out of his chair, dead. This was the only time in my life I could not shed a tear but felt like I was choking to death. Grandpa Henry was born November 1st, 1836, and died July 6th, 1914. Grandma Sophia came back to live with us after his death. She was born March 3rd, 1836, and died November 13th, 1918.

Back at that time, Papa kept hogs and raised pigs to butcher for family use. He killed the hogs at home, and neighbors came to help in the fall when the weather turned cold enough to salt the meat down so it would not spoil. They had a big iron kettle to render fat down to make lard. A fire was built outside, and when the fat was finished it was poured through a strainer and the cracklin's were kept to put in the corn bread.

They raised all kinds of vegetables for home use, and we never knew anything about going hungry or going without food. We had so many beans of so many kinds to pick in the fall. Papa had a bank barn, and he poured many a sack of beans on the barn floor and would take frails when the beans were dried in the hull and frail them. The beans would be piled under the hulls, and we had to take the hulls off and gather the beans. They would be put in a wheat fan that had a tray like a sifter, and it cleaned the trash out of the beans. We had bags of shelled beans to eat, and we sold a lot at three cents per pound. The money helped buy our fall and winter clothes.

We also had a chestnut orchard, and we would pick up two- and three-gallon buckets full of chestnuts in a short time. Papa would fill a two-bushel sack and get on his horse and take them to Montebello and sell them.

In 1915, Mama got real sick, and the doctors said she had Bright's disease, which is a kidney infection. Papa was good at nursing sickness, so Mama got over that attack. What her real problem was, she was a diabetic, and no doctor at that time knew how to treat her for that. They didn't know about diabetes, and Mama got pregnant and had our youngest sister, Mabel, on July 2, 1918. Mama died on October 16 of that year, when Mabel was three and a half months old. This left Papa, Grandma Sophia, William, myself, Claiborne, Velma, and baby Mabel at home. Not any of the family knew how to mix the formula for Mabel, but Papa had been making it and continued to do so, but the baby was not getting along well. Papa said that Mama's voice came to the foot of his bed one night and told him how to mix Mabel's formula. He did what she said, and baby Mabel began to do real good.

People back then had corn shuckings at night, and neighbors came to help each other get their corn in. As it happened, Harper, my brother-in-law, was having such a gathering at their barn on November 13, 1918. Papa had come home, and it was bed time. Grandma Sophia had already gone up to bed, and I went up soon after Papa came in. We found that she had died that quick after going to bed. It was a little less than a month from the time that Mama died. This was so hard on our dad, to lose a wife and a grandma. Grandma

School children at Peter Spring School

The Childhood Memories of Lora Ethel Fitzgerald Allen Matheny

Sophia was like his own mother, for she took him when he was two years old and raised him until he was married.

That fall, William went back to a two-room schoolhouse at Peter Spring, and the next fall, he left home and went to Fork Union Military Academy. He never came home to stay after he left that time. Claiborne went to live with our sister Pearl, so Velma, Mabel, and Papa stayed at home. Soon after, I left to live with my sister Lottie, who lived near Eagle Rock. I had been dating Eugene Montgomery Allen, the man I married, for seven months, so we decided to get married on July 14, 1920, at Salt Peter Cave, Virginia. Eugene and his brother Leslie had bought a farm, so we went there to live the day after we were married. We lived there until September and found the land was no good to farm. Eugene came to South River Lumber Company and got a job, so we sold our farm and moved to Round Hill, and the lumber company furnished us with a two-room shanty to live in. When we moved in, I was happy, for everything looked nice. We didn't have much furniture but enough for what we needed. Then Eugene's brother Claude came to live with us, and we sent him to school where Beulah Fauber was the teacher.

Papa came to see us and brought Mabel to stay a few days, for they didn't get to come to our wedding. Eugene was working for four dollars per day, and we had been married for two months when I found I was pregnant with our

Eugene and Ethel after marriage

son Dennis. I had no one to tell me about pregnancy except my mother's sister, and she lived not far from us; so I told her I was pregnant, and I got help from her. Back then, teenagers didn't know a lot about sex like they do now. Our parents never talked about sex to us, and I was plain dumb about it before marriage. My married sister told me a few things just a week before I was married.

We moved from Round Hill to the Tye River on Durham's Run in January of 1921, and Dennis was born there on June 10th. Aunt Martha Ann Bradley was the midwife, and I got along good. She stayed with me all night, and when she went home, my grandmother came and stayed several days since by then my own mother had died.

Ethel and her second son, Glenn, at their Durham's Run home

We moved to Papa's tenant house that September, and I kept Mabel in the daytime so Velma could go to school. When school was out, we rented a house from Uncle Tom Bradley, Mama's brother, which was just on the hill above Fork Mountain schoolhouse where I had gone to school and got my education.

The Childhood Memories of Lora Ethel Fitzgerald Allen Matheny 183

Ethel with three of her children: Glenn, Louise, and Maxie

Note: Ethel and Eugene had five children, and their birth order is as follows: Harold Dennis, Glenn Harris, Louise Burgess, Eugene Maxie, and Verna Mae. At this writing, only Maxie survives.

The stately Elk Hill home

19

Elk Hill

It stands stately and proud on top of a large island in the South Rockfish Valley, overlooking fertile farmland and the blue mountains beyond. This "island" is referred to by geologists as a monadnock. Samuel Reid constructed his home and several of the outbuildings there circa 1749, and the family lived there until the end of the century. All that remains is a pile of stones and bricks behind the current Elk Hill residence. During my research at the National Register of Historic Places, I found is a wealth of information, more detailed than what I am able to print in *Crazy Quilt*. It can be viewed at https://www.dhr.virginia.gov/historic-registers/nelson-county.

Elk Hill, which is located along the Rockfish Valley Highway near Nellysford, Virginia, is one of the earliest existing farms in Nelson County and has served continuously as a farm for over 250 years, witnessing the rise and decline of both tobacco and apple farming in the Rockfish Valley.

Elk Hill was first settled by Alexander Reid and his son, Samuel Reid, in the mid-eighteenth century. In 1805, Hawes Coleman, the first of a long line of Coleman owners, bought the property and started the cultivation of tobacco.

The sign at the home's entrance

The rural farm is characterized by verdant fields, woodlands, and bottomland, with the South Fork of the Rockfish River and Reid's Creek on its northern, western, and eastern boundaries. It is surrounded by the Blue Ridge Mountains and retains its historic rural character. The entire farm, with its historical outbuildings, was placed on the National Register of Historic Places in 2007. The southern boundary of the farm is marked by an original mid-eighteenth century rock wall which runs along the property line. Route 151 divided the property when the road was built in 1936.

The main house sits atop a bluff in the center of the farm and faces south, overlooking the bottomlands. This bluff is called a monadnock, which, according to *Webster's Dictionary*, is a residual hill standing well above the surface of a surrounding plain or valley. The rear of the house faces north towards Devil's Knob, Black Rock Mountain, and Three Ridges Mountain and overlooks bottomland along the Rockfish River.

The original portion of the house was built between 1790 and 1810, according to Colonial Williamsburg. The home is now a substantial two-story, three-bay-wide dwelling with a central hall. Its construction features original post and beam framing with heart poplar clapboard siding. The two exterior-end brick chimneys have been stuccoed over, and the house rests upon a full English basement that is three or four feet above grade. The exterior door to the basement, complete with string latch, is still there.

The interior of Elk Hill reflects the many changes and additions that occurred during five generations of Coleman family ownership. After 1825, the house underwent a series of expansions and remodelings, done in the Greek revival style, and it was during this period that it acquired a U-shape floor plan.

The house largely assumed its current appearance resulting from a series of additions in 1902, when then owner Arthur T. Ewing (a Coleman family member) remodeled and enlarged it. At the same time, the kitchen wing was added, and an interior hall was created, which made the floor plan rectangular. The roof was raised to cover it over. A grand entrance portico was added, giving the house a stately image and making it a landmark in Nelson County. The present house and contributing outbuildings are in excellent condition.

A 1937 photo of Elk Hill (Courtesy of the National Archives)

Arthur T. Ewing, standing by a Norton Pippin apple tree, 1902
(Courtesy of Virginia Department of Historic Resources)

In 1955, the owners, Ed and Marion Kyle, commissioned Charlottesville architect Milton Grigg to update and enlarge Elk Hill, adding a bedroom wing and modern conveniences. The house was heated by wood until 1955.

Elk Hill left the Coleman family's ownership when it was bought by current owners Peter and Betsy Agelasto in 1978.

Today, under the Agelasto ownership, the house reflects many modern updates, including satellite hookup, multi-zoned air conditioning and heating, and state-of-the-art appliances. The interior and exterior of the house, however, basically remain unchanged from the 1955 Grigg renovation. In the 1980s, Peter planted a vineyard; he successfully bottled and sold wine under the Elk Hill label for over fifteen years. In 2005, the Agelastos bought the neighboring

The Agelasto family: (L-R), son, Peter; Betsy; son, Parker, with Cooper (the dog); and Peter Sr. with their donkey, "Lilly of the Rockfish Valley"

property, which had originally been part of Elk Hill acreage. That same year, they put the Elk Hill land in conservation easement with the Virginia Outdoors Foundation to protect its natural habitats and rural character for the future. Elk Hill continues to be an active farm inhabited by cattle and three donkeys.

The outbuildings are some of the earliest structures on the property, including a circa 1790–1810 Prizery (tobacco-packing shed) with its original tobacco press. The large iron screw on the press replaced an earlier wooden one. This structure is unique in that there is not another like it in Nelson County or all of Virginia, according to Colonial Williamsburg.

The Prizery (early tobacco-packing shed)

There is also a circa 1790–1810 smoke house with its original wooden salting tray, a two-holer outhouse, a 1902 garage built to house the first Ewing automobile, and a two-car garage that was built closer to the house in 1955. A double-crib barn constructed in the nineteenth century was built with hand-hewn logs with V notches. According to state records, Hawes Coleman owned the home at a time when he

Tobacco press and large hogshead barrel

owned over two hundred slaves, which suggests that the barn was built by slave labor.

A rock boundary retaining wall, from rocks out of the fields as they were cleared, was built during the last quarter of the eighteenth century and runs along the original 1774 southern boundary between land owned by Alexander and Samuel Reid and the land owned by Alexander's first cousin, Andrew Reid.

A pile of chimney stones and bricks located behind the main house are from the ruins of the eighteenth-century dwelling built by Samuel Reid, who purchased five hundred acres in 1749, adjoining his cousin Alexander's seven hundred acres. The dwelling was still standing in the twentieth century and was occupied by house servants.

An ice house site was located northeast of the main house and was demolished in the 1950s.

Early smoke house

A nineteenth-century shed that was used for storing Delco batteries to create power for lighting was torn down in the 1990s, as was a chicken house.

An 1860s office used by Dr. Hawes Coleman for his medical practice was taken down at an earlier time. It stood on the east side of the main house. Other interesting sites on the

1902 Ewing garage

Nineteenth-century double-crib barn

Elk Hill property are the remains of an eighteenth-century cabin and a cemetery. The stone foundation and chimney remnants of the cabin dwelling are located in the woods west of the barn and are believed to be part of the first residence Andrew Reid built in the 1740s. The cabin was occupied into the twentieth century.

Elk Hill Cemetery, no longer a part of Elk Hill property, is a former slave cemetery. It was begun in the eighteenth century and is located in the woods west of the old cabin remains. Early rough fieldstone markers are still visible, as well as later burial sites with small ground markers. Several local African American families continue to bury their family members here. There are in excess of one hundred graves located on the over two-acre site. It is thought that there may have been an early church located near the graveyard and may have burned down. The land for the present Elk Hill Baptist Church on Glenthorne Loop was gifted by the Ewing family, and many of its members are associated with this cemetery.

Elk Hill was one of seven houses, located within a mile of each other, that were built near the community of Nellysford between the late eighteenth and early nineteenth centuries. Still standing today are River Bluff (c. 1775), Wintergreen (c. 1789), Glenthorne (c. 1840), and High View, now called Mill Hill (c. 1834). Valleymont (c. 1850) and Glen Mary (c. 1840) have been lost to demolition or neglect. All of these estates were working farms. Glenthorne and Elk Hill are the only ones that currently operate as farms.

Rear view of Glenthorne, c. 1840

These late eighteenth- and early nineteenth-century properties are part of the South Rockfish Valley Rural Historic District, recognized by the Virginia Department of Historic Resources and the US Department of Interior for their history of agriculture, architecture, and commerce—"a well preserved example of a rural agricultural area" with a continuous use of more than 250 years of farming, beginning with tobacco, later with apples, and today with grapes, apples, hops, and cattle. Today's farming industry has brought with it the development of wineries and cideries.

In 2000, Al Weed, Carrie Whitehead, and Peter Agelasto attended a meeting at the Lovingston courthouse. They sat next to Karen Firehook, who told them she had a funding source to do a watershed forum. She asked if they knew anyone who wanted to compete for the grant. The three of them talked it over, and, that night, they created the Rockfish Watershed Forum. At the forum, John McClain, who attended for the Virginia Department of Transportation, stood and asked if there was an area where VDOT could restore a stream as a mitigation project. During the break, Peter talked to him about the possibility of restoring the South Fork of the Rockfish River that was irreparably damaged during Hurricane Camille. It had been rebuilt by the Corps of Army Engineers but had failed. A two-mile reconstruction of the river between Moses Hughes Road and Reid's Creek, part of which ran through Elk Hill, was accepted by VDOT.

It took about five years for the engineering and construction to take place. During that time, the Agelastos placed the farm in conservation easements with the Virginia Outdoors Foundation. Another outcome of the forum was the establishment of the Friends of the Rockfish Watershed.

I asked Peter what the work involved, and he said, "VDOT approached the mitigation with the latest scientific stream-restoration knowledge, adding numerous rock structures to protect the banks and to slow the flow of the river." This was an experimental project and would be treated as a learning experience. Within ten years, some of the structures failed; after more studies, VDOT revised some of their previous work, and it looks to be successful.

Around the time the original river work was being done, the federal government promoted a program to help farmers fence their land to keep the cattle out of the streams. After the pastures were fenced and alternative water sources were created on the farm, the Agelasto family decided to open a trail system along the Rockfish River for the public to enjoy. It was one of the first times public trails had been put on private property. Peter hired Chris Gensic, now director of trails for the City of Charlottesville, to layout and design the trails, which extend for six miles through private lands and are now used extensively.

In 2005, Peter and Betsy created the Rockfish Valley Foundation (www.rockfishvalley.org). Its goal is to get people, both young and old, outdoors and to promote the understanding of the natural elements, past and present cultures, and the history of Nelson County. With the help of friends

Breathtaking view at the trail head

and volunteers, the foundation has grown over the years and now includes the South Rockfish River Trail System, Spruce Creek Park and its Children's Nature Trail, and the Natural

History Center, which opened in 2012 in the old Wintergreen Country Store.

The RVF also collaborates with the Nelson County schools. In addition, the RVF obtained a grant to locate a historical marker about the Hurricane Camille destruction in the South Rockfish Valley of Nelson County. The marker was erected at the trail head parking area on the site of the

The Natural History Center in old Wintergreen village

Ed Ewing house, which had been destroyed during the storm and where Ed and his wife had lost their lives.

The interview came to a close as Peter, Betsy, and I finished talking over a cup of Earl Grey tea at the kitchen table. The Agelastos are such fine people, warm and knowledgeable and willing to share that knowledge with those interested in learning more about Nelson County and Virginia's early history. They have always been so helpful to me personally, and I thank them for their part in preserving Elk Hill's invaluable history and keeping the rural flavor of Nelson County alive and ongoing.

20

"OCD"

I had never thought of myself as having Obsessive-Compulsive Disorder until a teenager in my class at Vacation Bible School pointed out that I was micromanaging a photo collage that the kids were supposed to be making. I was placing all the pictures in a perfect mosaic pattern. What she said was, "How long have you had OCD?" I had no idea what she was talking about until I came home and looked it up. No *wonder* I loved watching the television program *Monk*; although, thank the good Lord, I'm not quite at stage four of the disease as he was. A stage two, maybe.

I guess I come by it honestly. My dad used to drive all the relatives crazy with remarks like, "Do you know how many steps it is from our front door to the mailbox?" Or, "You can shave a half-mile off your trip to the grocery store by taking a left on thirty-third street instead of a right." When everyone else was rolling their eyes up into their heads and groaning, I was paying attention. He also kept all the screwdrivers lined up together in his toolbox, and each size nail had its own compartment in the little plastic pull-out drawers he kept on the shelf in the garage.

I well remember the exact spot on the highway when my dad turned to me and said, "Always remember this is where our Dodge Dart's odometer turned 100,000 miles." I never forgot. It was out by the landfill on Dixie Highway when I was in the eleventh grade. I find myself doing the same thing now; our little Honda CRV turned 200,000 miles just past David Hatter's house on Love Road. My long-suffering husband resisted the urge to roll his eyes into his head and groan.

Looking back, I've always had the urge to straighten crooked pictures hanging on a wall or put flower pots exactly in the middle of the porch posts. My biggest OCD moment always comes at the end of the harvest season when I organize the canned goods by color on the shelves in my pantry. The reds of canned tomatoes always go next to the whites of sauerkraut, never beside the pickled beets—not enough definition between the colors. I've always thought this was perfectly normal and not a brain defect.

While I'm thinking about it, my mother had her own personal fetish about the linen closet. All the green sheets were lined up together, and the blue towels were alternated with the pink, giving an overall pleasing effect when the door was opened. Kind of feng shui for the closet. With both parents exhibiting this type of behavior, it was a given I'd follow in their footsteps.

Although I do like things orderly, I'm not driven to distraction, say, if the grass is cut in any particular pattern as I see at some homes. Ever notice those perfect diagonal cuts in yards where men are out there on riding lawnmowers? OCD, I betcha! There are more of us around than not.

I have no medical proof as to whether this oddity is hereditary or just a learned behavior, but my daughter organizes her shirts by sleeveless, short/long sleeves, turtlenecks, and vests, and her sock drawer is a thing of beauty with all the rolled-up sausages in perfect symmetry. At the age of two, her daughter would compulsively reorganize the candy and gum rack while sitting in a cart at the grocery checkout line.

So our entire family lineage is doomed to have type-A, anal-retentive habits.

While reading my column to Billy, he said not to forget to mention that I always put exactly twenty-six pieces of wood in the wheelbarrow when coming from the woodpile to the back porch. He says, "What does it matter?" I say, "Give me a break, it's what I can comfortably push; plus twenty-six is such a nice round number!"

I once read a story in *Reader's Digest* about a young man who had the habit of tapping out a certain rhythm with a pencil eraser. The thing drove him (and everyone else) crazy for years. One day, he had a car accident, hitting his head so hard it left him unconscious for a few days. When he awoke, the compulsion had left him, and he tapped no more. With that said, I pray for safety so I may continue to line up the Ball jars in my pantry in traditional OCD color-coordinated fashion.

Canned blackberry juice

21

Homemade Blackberry Juice

Back in the 1980s, while delivering the *Backroads* newspaper, I stopped at Freddie and Hazel Phillips's house in Nellysford, and Hazel offered me a glass of cold grape juice. It was the best I'd ever tasted, and I asked if it was hard to make. Hazel laughed and told me she had a very easy recipe that was fail-safe and wrote it down for me before I left. She said to make it go a little further, she often mixed it half and half with either ginger ale or Wink, a carbonated grapefruit soda. Sure enough, the recipe was super easy, and that September I picked grapes at a local vineyard and made about ten gallons, packed in half-gallon jars. We drank it throughout the winter months, and when I served it to guests, they all raved how great it tasted. It is now a standard request at Thanksgiving and Christmas at the Coffey household.

Fast forward twenty years, and I'm still making the same recipe, except with a slightly different twist; this year I experimented with an excess of the blackberries that grow on our property. We were surprised to have stumbled on a tart and delicious drink that can't be found in most grocery stores. Our blackberries are the thornless, domestic kind, given to us as slips by Phillip Greene of Tyro many years ago. They aren't as sweet as the wild berries, but for jelly and cobbler they are fine; and this year we've found a brand-new use for them as well.

Here is Hazel's grape juice recipe that has stood the test of time. Add one cup of sugar to two cups of stemmed whole grapes in a half-gallon Mason jar that has been heated in boiling water. Fill the jar with boiling water, wipe the rim, put on the lid and screw top that have also been in the hot water, and tighten down. That's it!

Boiling the half-gallon jars

Put the jar in a dark place (mine's in our kitchen pantry; Hazel's was in her basement) and leave as long as you can stand not to drink it. The longer it sits, the stronger and better the taste. For grape juice, I make it mid-September and *try* not to sample it before Thanksgiving. For the blackberry juice, I left the first batch for only two weeks before trying it simply to see if it was going to be worth using all my berry crop on. It was tangy and good in two weeks, so sitting for a few months should ripen it perfectly.

Homemade Blackberry Juice

Filling hot jars with sugar

Adding the berries to the sugar

Pouring boiling water into the jars

Removing the bubbles before capping

One difference between the two juices is that with the grapes, I picked a bushel at the vineyard, came home, and made everything in one day. The blackberries ripened at different times, so I made the juice kind of piecemeal, a few gallons at a time; or I froze all the berries and made the juice all at once. Also, I added a cup and a half of sugar instead of just a cup for the grape recipe because of the tartness of the blackberries.

When the juice is first made, the berries float to the top of the jar. After two weeks, they drop to the bottom. And, as another experiment, after we drank the juice, I used the sugar-infused berries to make a blackberry cobbler! How's that for a "two-fer"? The final product was delightful, unique, and quite delicious!

Blackberry cobbler from the "leftovers"

For a simple cobbler recipe, I use the one Hallie Henderson gave me almost forty years ago. Melt a half stick of butter in a square (8" x 8") baking pan. Mix together one cup of sugar, one cup of regular flour, one cup of milk, and two teaspoons of baking powder in a bowl and pour over the melted butter. Add the leftover berries (or a cup or so of any other fruit) and pop in the oven at 350 degrees for thirty-five to forty-five minutes or until brown on top and a toothpick inserted in the middle comes out clean. Simple, easy, and oh, so good!

Russell in the doorway of his root cellar

22

Russell Lowery's Root Cellar

Russell Lowery chose the perfect spot to build his house at the bottom of Love, Virginia, nestled in a small flat between two mountain ridges and bordering Back Creek. Russell bought the nine acres of land known as the Lambert Place in 1989 and began construction of the home in 1990, moving in about a year later.

The finished ground house

In 1995, he decided to dig out a section of a small rise on the lower side of the main road for a root cellar, or ground house, as many of the native people call them. Before the onset of electricity, most people living in the Blue Ridge had root cellars in which to store their harvest. They were located close to the family home, making foodstuffs easily accessible for a meal.

Typically, a cellar was dug into the side of a mountain or hill, although Maynard Patterson of Sherando built his on flat land and heaped dirt around three sides, and it serves the same purpose.

Maynard Patterson by his root cellar, Sherando

Interiors had dirt floors and walls that were lined with rocks found on the property. A roof was built over the exterior, and dirt was piled on top; this allowed vegetation to take root, which controlled erosion. A stout wooden door was placed at the entrance to keep out cold winter air. Many times, a screen door was added to allow summer breezes to ventilate the inside, reducing moisture and letting the cellar breathe. The inside was kept at a year-round temperature of about fifty-five degrees, making it cool in the summer and warm in the winter. Wooden shelves were constructed to hold a variety of canned goods. Crocks and barrels were also used to store everything from apple butter to sauerkraut. Bins held potatoes, turnips, and apples.

Russell dug the hole for his root cellar with a Caterpillar front-end loader; eight courses of cinderblock were laid on the sides and backfilled with dirt. Sidney Ray Shirley helped Russell lay the block, and Donnie "Duck" Coffey, an up-the-road neighbor living on Campbell's Mountain Road, donated three locust trees about fourteen inches in diameter for the center and side posts. For the roof, wooden boards were nailed on, keeping an old-time look. To keep the boards from rotting, sheets of one-eighth-inch galvanized metal was laid on the boards before Russell put the dirt on top.

The cellar's finished size is about ten by fourteen feet. Creosoted railroad ties were laid on the sides and across the front, lending more protection from moisture. Natural rock

Early stone foundation

taken from an old foundation adjacent to the cellar was used to face the entrance. Bobby Henderson, who lives on the property next to Lowery, donated a wooden door and came to help put it on. Inside, three wooden shelves on each side hold all the glass canning jars filled with the various foodstuffs that Russell cans each year from his large garden.

A large plastic barrel mounted on the back wall holds loose apples bought from Tommy Fitzgerald's orchard in Tyro each autumn. The barrel has a door cut in the side that can be opened to put the apples in and can be shut to keep the mice from snacking on the fruit. In the fall months, Russell makes a large kettle of apple butter that he cans and stores in the cellar and gives as gifts to friends.

Interior of Russell's cellar

He does the same with the hog meat that he butchers every year, gracing friends with homemade sausage. He smiled and said, "I've got a lot of Charlene in me." He was raised up in the "Frog Hollow" section of Stuarts Draft, and his mother, Charlene, was the one who taught him to cook, can, and always share with others. Russell has incorporated a full working kitchen into his basement; this is where he does all his canning and butchering work. Russell is a boilermaker by trade, and many times during the weekdays, he was working in other states. He said it took about a month to complete the cellar construction due to just working on the weekends.

The Lowery ground house is a thing of beauty with its rock face and inside shelves stocked with canned goods. Tomatoes, green beans, sauerkraut, pickles, salsa, and everything in between stands ready for hearty and healthy eating.

An array of canned goods

Russell retired in 2008 and now has more time to pursue the things he enjoys, such as fishing. He is also a bear hunter, and during the winter months, he participates in this long-standing traditional sport of Virginia mountain men. His children visit often, and the grandchildren clearly love their granddaddy and enjoy fishing in the large pond on the property. Two wild geese and their brood of five goslings,

Matt Hatter's cellar, Campbell's Mountain

as well as two female mallard ducks, make their home here, following Russell around, hoping for a handout of corn, with which he willingly obliges them.

People now shop weekly for fresh fruits and vegetables at grocery stores or local farmer's markets, but in years past, root cellars played an important part of food preservation for the mountain people of Virginia.

Russell Lowery is an example of a younger

Bobby Henderson's ground house, Love

man who values the older traditions and has incorporated those traditions into his own life, keeping the old-time ways of his parents and grandparents alive and vital in this modern-day world.

The cellar at Maphis Campbell's home, Beech Grove

Mitchael Seaman's two-story cellar, Fork Mountain

Beech Grove Christian Church

23

Beech Grove Christian Church

This invaluable early history of Beech Grove Church was given to me in 2001 by Jerry Campbell, who was raised in the community. I published it in the *Backroads* newspaper but felt it deserved to be included in *Crazy Quilt* because the detailed information needed to be more permanently preserved. My special thanks to Jerry, who graciously shared a part of history that might have been forgotten. In 2019, Beech Grove Church will celebrate its 144th anniversary.

INTRODUCTION BY JERRY CAMPBELL

I have retyped [the following] 100-year history of Beech Grove Christian Church from a copy given to me by my aunt, Thelma Campbell Leech. I do not know who wrote the original version, and I cannot make any claim as to the correctness of the information. My mother, Margaret Campbell, thinks Miss Beulah Fitzgerald has a book containing the history of the church, but the book disappeared after her death. Perhaps someone living in the Beech Grove community or attending the church knows something of that book.

My family moved to Beech Grove in 1944 after my grandmother, Laura Dodd Campbell, died. Some of my earliest memories are of attending services at the church that stood in what is now part of the church cemetery on Cub Creek Road. I remember Mr. Clarence Campbell serving as Sunday School Superintendent. He was a very tall, imposing figure of a man. I especially remember the lawn parties that were enjoyed by all on the church lawn each summer. Mr. Tom Quick would always make lemonade in my grandmother's twenty-gallon crock, which I have in my home today. I remember going to Waynesboro with my uncle, Irving Campbell, to get ice cream and ice. The ice cream would be packed in dry ice to keep it from melting, and we would wrap the blocks of ice in tarps to keep it clean and reduce melting.

I accepted Christ at a 1951 revival in which J. T. Watson was preaching. I was baptized in the river flowing through Beech Grove. The "wash hole" was used for baptizing, and this was located across the road from where Mrs. Melba Fields lives today. Many of the people mentioned in this history were familiar to me as I grew up in the community. I married in 1959 and moved to Waynesboro and lost touch with a lot of people living in Beech Grove. There are some folks not mentioned in this history that I know gave of their time, talents, and finances for the betterment of the church. Some that come to mind are: Pearl Smith Campbell (wife of Clarence and later married to Tom Quick), Nanny Campbell (wife of Palmer), Dorothy Ellinger Thompson (wife of Worthy), Lawney Fitzgerald (who served as Sunday School Superintendent), Donald Falls (who also served as Superintendent), Ruth Shirley McGann (wife of Luther), and Stanley McGann. Dorothy Thompson and Nanny Campbell were Sunday school teachers of mine in the 1940s and 1950s.

I hope this recorded written history will be distributed to the members of Beech Grove Church today, and they will have an appreciation of what has taken place over the last 125 years.

—*Jerry Campbell, September 4, 2001*

HISTORY AS SUBMITTED BY THELMA CAMPBELL LEECH

The earliest records of Beech Grove Church have been lost over the years, but much information has been preserved, both orally and in written form from its senior members.

Services were conducted prior to 1875 in a grove of beech trees in the open, according to data found on a card that was placed in a small book, *Methodist Hymns*, that had been used by John W. Lockridge in services he apparently led. Harry Hughes had given this book to the church. Later, the meetings were held in an old building located near the home of Sallie McGann. From these early gatherings, Beech Grove Christian Church was formed.

Early congregation at original church

Determined from facts found by Beulah Fitzgerald and the Rev. J. T. Watson, in an 1880s church newspaper called *The Atlantic Missionary*, the files are now in the University of Virginia archives in Charlottesville, Virginia. These files state that the church at Beech Grove was founded in 1875. The Rev.

Z. Parker Richardson of Louisa, Virginia, organized the first church, and he preached there on and off for thirty-five years.

Mrs. Ernest Fields recalls hearing her parents, the late Mr. and Mrs. P. S. Dodd, speak of the three ministers in their early life at the church: Rev. Z. Parker Richardson, Walter S. Hoye, and C. R. Perry. These men traveled throughout the Piedmont District of churches, holding revivals and preaching at irregular intervals, and it was in one of these services that young Martha Dodd accepted Christ as her Savior. It was a while before any preacher returned for another service, and when the day came for the young girl's baptism, the weather had turned cold and ice had to be broken on a pond before she could be immersed. The last record of a service held by Rev. Richardson was in 1910.

Brother H. Davis Coffey writes in his biography: "The Beech Grove Christian Church was organized many years ago by Walter Hoye and Parker Richardson. An old store building was used as a church and I preached in that building several times before we decided to erect a church building. The walls went up because the people had a mind to work. We worked almost three weeks before it was completed and seated. I walked more than a thousand miles across the high point of the Blue Ridge Mountains to preach for that church for a

Rev. H. Davis Coffey

period of eight years and received three dollars for the job of building the church, preaching and visiting. I did not ask for that much. Some splendid people live in that section."

Records show the parcel of land on which the church was built was donated by W. R. Rodes and is very near the site of the present Beech Grove Church. At this time, the church was given the name of Union Church and was used both by the Baptists and Disciples of Christ. Later, the Baptists ceased to use it, and it became the soul [sic] property of the Disciples. They worshipped there from 1888 until 1916, when the building fell into disrepair.

Rev. J. T. Watson and Joseph Coffey

Mrs. Ernest Fields writes again in her memoirs, "My first remembrance of church life was a one-room building a few yards from our present church. Rev. Abner C. Knibb was one of the active ministers at this time and baptized me in 1911."

In 1915, the Beech Grove Junior High School was built, and after the above-mentioned church could no longer be used for worship, the people were given permission to hold services in the auditorium of the school. Rev. J. T. Watson was one who came to preach at Beech Grove in 1915. It is told that he went to the mountains and helped cut logs to build the new school. He came many times to preach and held many revivals over a period of years in three different Beech Grove Church buildings.

The marker at Beech Grove Cemetery

No one could find a written record of charter members, but with the help of older members, it was found that some of these were: William Dodd (known as Uncle Billy), Jack Hughes, Martha Dodd, Lawson Campbell, Jetsel Fitzgerald, Mary A. Dodd, Alec Dodd, Robert Fields, Napoleon "Po" Fitzgerald, Myra Dodd, and Patrick S. Dodd, also known as "Pete."

After four years of holding worship services in the school auditorium, the group moved one Sunday morning in 1920 to a new church that had been purchased from the Dunkards. This was located on the land where Beech Grove Christian Church Cemetery now stands on Cub Creek Road.

At the time of the move, the Rev. Alfred E. Sims was the minister. From all that could recall, he was known as a fine organizer, and the congregation grew and progressed rapidly. A. C. Knibb came frequently to hold services. Also listed as ministers were W. H. Leake and Alvin Reynolds.

Grave markers in the cemetery

One of the stories told of the early days was that the church was not just there for Disciple ministers to preach and teach the word of God to the people, but several Presbyterian ministers were welcomed into the church to hold services and to help in whatever way possible. One of these men, Rev. Profitt, was instrumental in building the present-day Beech Grove Church for the Presbyterians, but the denomination didn't grow in the community, and it wasn't long until the minister had no flock of his own and came to preach to the Disciples on occasion.

One story about loving and serving is told of the late Jim Thompson (father of Londie Thompson, now deceased, and grandfather of Worthy Thompson and Mrs. Blanche Fields), who brought unleavened cakes of bread that had been baked by his wife for each Lord's Day Communion service at the church. He walked to the church each Sunday for many years, performing this service for the ongoing of the church. There were also many others who made the work of the church an intricate part of their lives.

Tombstone of Mary Elizabeth Fitzgerald

H. Glenn Haney served Beech Grove Church for some time, and many members have fond memories of him. R. Lee Sadler also came from Lynchburg for irregular intervals of preaching until his health broke completely.

John McKinney was called as pastor in 1936 and served for ten years, working with Wintergreen Christian Church as well as Beech Grove.

Early photo of Wintergreen Christian Church

On Sunday, January 9, 1944, the late Clarence Campbell announced that he wanted the members to start a building fund for a new church. Maphis Campbell recalled that there were only six people attending the morning service that day. They were: Tom Quick, Londie Thompson, Palmer Campbell, Irving Campbell, Clarence Campbell, and Maphis Campbell. These faithful men had come to church in snow that was extremely deep. Clarence had ridden his horse from where he lived, and the snow was up to the horse's stomach. But enthusiasm was as great as the snow, and the collection of ten dollars was the beginning of the building fund. Since that day was the second Sunday of the month, each second Sunday thereafter was designated "building fund Sunday."

In late summer of 1944, M. Met Hughes, a Beech Grove native, now deceased, showed his interest in the building program by offering the church five-hundred dollars, provided the people could raise an equal amount by November 12, 1944. A committee was appointed which consisted of Mrs. Ernest Fields, Sallie McGann, and Margaret Campbell, and these three ladies were to canvas the community and friends for the matching five-hundred dollars. They exceeded their goal by $56.37. It was six years of faithful and loving sacrifice by the members of the church, along with donations by other church members in and out of the state, that finally brought about the dream come true. In July of 1950, the sum of $5,622.81 had been raised, and the present building was purchased for $3,800.00. Built of native stone, the church had been known as Hudson Memorial Presbyterian Church, organized in about 1922, and was later used as a private residence.

In January of 1951, remodeling began under the capable supervision of Londie Thompson. In nine months' time, donations came in from many sources, and $7,576.37 was on hand for the work in progress. Again, as many years before, H. D. Coffey said of the people at Beech Grove, "They were of a mind to work," and the members gave many hours of hard work.

The church was dedicated on September 9, 1951, and about six-hundred people, from near and far, gathered to celebrate that special Sunday. Not the least of the drawing cards was the bountiful and excellent food served for lunch. The Rev. Kenneth Lambdin was pastor of the church at this time.

Interior of Beech Grove Church sanctuary

J. T. Watson, former pastor of the church, gave the dedication address, followed by the act of dedication by the pastor and congregation. Robert Whitehead, Nelson County Delegate to the Virginia House of Delegates, gave the "Afternoon Challenge." The service closed with the singing of the hymn, "Blest Be the Tie That Binds." After the dedication, there was still much work to be done by the congregation as followers of Jesus Christ as $3,000 was still needed to pay off the balance owed on church furnishings, heating, and other church-related items. This amount was borrowed for a ten-year period but again, with donations being made by so many, both in and outside the church, it was only three years before the note was paid in full and the church was debt free.

E. Elwood Campbell was pastor at this time. He was studying for the ministry and was serving both Wintergreen and Beech Grove Church. The note burning took place on February 14, 1954. Maphis Campbell, in giving his tribute to the church that Sunday, stated: "It shows what organization and leadership combined with love and the desire for a better place to worship can do. In memory of the late Clarence Campbell, who had the vision of a new church and the initiative to launch a building fund, and Uncle Billy Dodd, P. S. Dodd, H. D. Fitzgerald, M. C. Campbell, Otis McGann, J. D. Hughes, Luther McGann, along with our fathers and others, who down through the years served faithfully as Christian leaders and teachers in the community."

Under the leadership of Elwood Campbell, the church went through amazing changes for the better as far as structural organizing was concerned. Committees were formed that functioned quite efficiently, and they grew in many ways. He stressed the need for Sunday school classrooms, since all of the classes were being held in the sanctuary, and it was very confusing for all concerned. So, on February 3, 1954, a committee was formed to look into the prospects of classrooms. The members of this committee were: Basil Campbell, Irving Campbell, Jess Hughes, and Garth Fields. Elwood Campbell resigned from Beech Grove in 1956, and in July of 1957, the Rev. J. D. Farris was called to serve the Beech Grove/Wintergreen Field.

Along with ministering to the congregation and other pastoral duties, the pastor had also fallen heir to still another dream of the Beech Grove people: building classrooms. Rev. Farris was just the man to offer extraordinary help along these lines, being skilled in carpentry and planning.

In May of 1958, plans were drawn up by Rev. Farris and submitted to the congregation for approval and suggestions.

Members voted to accept the plans and go ahead with the building on Sunday, June 29, 1958. On the first Sunday in August, the trustees broke ground for the educational unit. The plans called for six classrooms in a semi-basement, two classrooms on the first floor, along with a kitchen, two bathrooms, and a baptistery. The work began and progressed rapidly; with the first floor near completion and with heating installed, it was possible to hold a Thanksgiving supper in November. The event brought in over four-hundred dollars in additional money to be paid on classroom expenses.

By May of 1959, the addition was nearing completion, and the cornerstone was laid on the last Sunday in May. The history of the church, names of officers, teachers, and the enrollment of the Sunday school and church were placed in a box, sealed permanently, and enclosed in the corner of the new building.

Dedication of the new addition was on the second Sunday in August 1959. Rev. Myron Kaufman was guest speaker for

The 1959 stone addition to the church

the occasion, and that same day Rev. Clarence Smoot began a week of revival services. Rev. Farris remained pastor until June of 1965 and resigned at that time for another field.

Ben Bohren came in September of 1966, a fresh young student from Lynchburg College and very able to cope with the young people needing a revitalized program. This young man did outstanding work with both Wintergreen and Beech Grove for two years and then left to go on to seminary at Lexington, Kentucky. Ken Paquin took up where Ben Bohren left off (he was also a student at Lynchburg College), and he was very capable and energetic, doing great work for the up-building of the church. But he, too, left us in May of 1971. At that time, Rev. Farris was called back to pastor Beech Grove, and at this time of writing he continues to serve.

Perhaps, as this history of the 100 years at Beech Grove Christian Church comes to a close, we should stop and think about the great legacy that has been left to us by our forefathers. There is a divine reason in the fact that when other denominations tried and failed in the community, the Disciples kept on through many trials and tribulations. Let us not be lacking in the strength that made the church have great meaning and promise for several generations. We have finished 100 years, but we also begin another era, and we cannot do less than has been done for us if we are to extend the same legacy to future generations.

—*Submitted by Thelma Campbell Leech*

PASTORS WHO SERVED AT BEECH GROVE

Z. Parker Richardson, Walter S. Hoye, C. R. Perry, H. Davis Coffey, Abner C. Knibb, Alfred Simms, Hoye Leake, Alvin Reynolds, Glenn Haney, Lee Sadler, John McKinney (1936–1946), Raymond Morgan (1946), Walter Bingham (1946–1948), J. T. Watson (1949–1950), Kenneth Lambdin (1950–1953), E. Elwood Campbell (1953–1956),

J. D. Farris (1957–1965), Benjamin Bohren (1966–1968), Kenneth Paquin (1968–1971), Rev. J. D. Farris, Earl Burch, James Lowe, Rhoads Artz, Don Gardner, Kaye Edwards, Linda Parker, Charlie Ellis, Ken Schuler, Ray Coffey, Ernie Love, Saylor J. "Billy" Coffey, and current pastor Mike Auen.

PASTORS WHO CONDUCTED REVIVALS

J. T. Watson, J. W. West, W. F. Shinell (a blind preacher, humorist, and lecturer), Miles Austin, J. D. Farris, H. Myron Kaufman, Barney Stephens, John Suttenfiled, Melvin Bobbitt, Alvin Reynolds, Clarence Smoot, Jack Hamilton, Danny Beard, Warren Burbaker, Jann Linn, James D. Lowe, E. Elwood Campbell, and Dennis Reynolds.

Note: Bud Quick told me his aunt, Sally Campbell, lived in the church when it was a private residence. It wasn't "quiet" enough for her, so she moved to the last house on the right side of the road, near the top of the mountain. The home burned down after she died. Also, a special thanks to Melba Fields, Ruth Shirley McGann, and Ollie Hughes for the information on the pastors.

Today, Beech Grove Christian Church continues to hold services and is a small but thriving congregation. Pastor Mike Auen has served the church for eleven years as of this writing and is loved by his flock. The church is nondenominational and welcomes visitors and those looking for a church home. Services include Sunday school at 9:45 a.m. and worship at 11:00 a.m. each Sunday morning, with a prayer meeting and dinner on the last Wednesday of each month at 6:15 p.m. Additional information may be obtained from Pastor Mike Auen at 540-241-2317.

Mike Auen, present pastor of Beech Grove

Mutt Humphreys, longtime logger

24

Mutt Humphreys— A Day in the Life of a Logger

Most people get up in the morning and head off to work with no thoughts of impending danger. In an office setting, getting a paper cut or having the computer down is a total inconvenience, but for the rugged men who make logging their profession, according to a new report from the Bureau of Labor Statistics, logging is the number one most dangerous occupation in the US, with commercial fishing coming in second.

For twenty-five years I was the publisher of a Virginia newspaper called *Backroads*, which featured many aspects of Appalachian culture. The November 2006 issue was dedicated solely to the men who made their living logging; after interviewing them, I had new respect for a trade that supplies wood products to the building and paper industry, as well as to hobbyists. One such man is Mutt Humphreys, who, at the time of the interview, was logging a large tract of land in Beech Grove, Virginia, owned by the Mansfield family.

Although Mutt has been logging full time only since 2002, he has been exposed to the industry all his life. His grandfather, Frank Humphreys, was one of the old-time timbermen from Montebello, Virginia. Mutt's father and his uncles were also involved in the logging trade, and, as a teenager, Mutt

Frank Humphreys astride his work horse

worked alongside them and found he loved working in the woods, but it wasn't until 2002 that he started logging for himself. Up to that time, he had worked twenty-one years for the Fairfield Bridge Company, first as a crane operator and later as an equipment superintendent, but he continued to log after work and on Saturdays. He made the decision to start logging full time after he got burned out on his former job.

When Mutt was in high school, he had an old ton truck and a McCulloch power saw, and he would go around and ask people if he could cut pine wood to clean up a piece of land. "I'd cut pulpwood and carry it out on my back, put it on the truck, and carry it down to Hector Taylor, who had a sawmill in Greenville, hoping to get fifty dollars a load."

When he went in business for himself, Mutt did logging, as well as excavating work. "I bought a track loader and would build roads and ponds for people but found out it was hard to collect for the work I'd done. It didn't take me long to get out of excavating. One nice thing about logging is that if you take a load to the saw mill, you'll get a check."

One of the biggest investments in the business is the equipment needed to do the job. Mutt started out buying a '71 Chevy truck that once belonged to a friend and an International front-end loader. He had an old track loader named

"Oscar" and added a 450-B John Deere dozer with a winch. Earlier in his career, he used Tree Farmer and Timberjack machinery but later went to all John Deere products. In the last year, he's updated his equipment to include a 540 cable skidder, a 648 grapple skidder, a 435 knuckleboom crane, an equipment trailer, and a Mack truck with a pup trailer. The pup trailer is pulled behind the truck and is capable of hauling more logs, making a bigger load.

Mutt tries to cut enough timber each day for a full load plus a few extra logs that, at the end of the week, will total an extra load in case the weather turns sour, and he can't work one day. Logging is fraught with setbacks, including wet and inclement weather, equipment breakdowns, and personal injury, which can bring work to a standstill. Mutt

Loggers Timmy and Mutt Humphreys, Jason Allen

can usually haul six thousand board feet in a load and says, "That's aplenty to cut in the mountains. I used to work from daylight to dark, but I don't do that anymore. You can't stand it. Physically, it takes its toll on your body."

In 2013, Jason Allen, who is also a certified electrician, began working with Mutt, saying that he, too, enjoys working in the out of doors. Jason started from scratch, but Mutt is quick to praise how quick he caught on to the trade and what a careful and experienced logger he's become, which is a necessity in a profession where your life is literally in your partner's hands. Mutt said he was glad Jason had never logged with anyone before, saying, "He didn't already have notions in his head of what to do, and I could teach him my way." Under Mutt Humphreys's careful mentorship, Jason has learned all the aspects of logging, and watching him and Mutt work together is like watching a perfectly choreographed dance with both men moving in sync.

In October 2017, Mutt's son, Timmy, came back on board full time and has been logging with his father and Jason ever since. Timmy was brought up in a logging family, and Mutt

Young logger, Timmy at fifteen

said he's been helping ever since he was big enough to get out in the woods. In the November 2006 *Backroads*, I interviewed Mutt for a special logging edition of the newspaper. At that time, Timmy was a fifteen-year-old sophomore at Riverheads High School, itching to graduate so he could log full time with his dad. After graduation, he did so for several years before finding other full-time employment but continued logging with Mutt on the weekends. But like

Timmy Humphreys by the JD skidder

so many men who grew up around the logging industry, it gets in their blood, and they eventually return to that type of work.

On a typical day, with no problems, Mutt, Jason, and Timmy head to the mountains where a skid road will be pushed out, and Mutt will start cutting and felling large trees. When a tree is on the ground, he will limb it up (cut the limbs off the trunk).

If the tree is down over the bank, Jason or Timmy will back the cable skidder as close to the tree as possible, unwind the cable, and attach it around the end of the tree so they can pull it out to a flat area. If the tree is easier to get to, Mutt will use the grapple skidder and just grab it. When enough trees are cut, the men will drag several together behind the

Pushing out a skid road

Mutt cutting a large poplar tree

two skidders and bring them down to a landing where Mutt measures each log according to length—sixteen, fourteen, ten, or eight feet—and spray-paints a mark across them, indicating where Jason and Timmy are to cut, which is called "bucking them up." The knuckleboom then lifts the logs and loads them onto the truck and trailer.

While some loggers use Stihl chain saws, all three men are strict Husqvarna users, and the larger saws cut through a butt log sixteen inches in diameter like soft butter.

Mutt looks at both small and large acreages, saying he's logged two-acre properties as well as two hundred. Asked what the most valuable wood is, he says walnut always brings top dollar, with oak next, and poplar being the most popular wood to cut. "It's easy; once it hits the ground, it basically has limbed itself."

Skidding logs out of the woods

Two different kinds of cuts loggers use to fell a tree are the "bird's mouth," or open face, and the hinge cut, which

Jason Allen bucking up logs to length

A knuckleboom crane lifting a log

is much safer. Using this method, a tree won't accidently split off at the stump and buck backwards, and it is the US Forest Service's recommended cut.

One of the hazards that makes logging the most dangerous profession is limbs coming off a cut tree as it hits other trees on its way down. This causes a boomerang effect, sometimes throwing limbs back at the logger. Mutt says that he tries not to cut on windy days, because you don't have control of the tree, and dropping limbs are a con-

Loading logs onto Mutt's truck

stant risk. Sometimes a cable will snap, and Mutt said he'd seen one snap and completely wrap around the skidder he was on. "I'm thankful for cages . . . cabs that protect you."

I asked if he'd ever gotten hurt logging, and he stated that he had been hit by one of the falling limbs and knocked senseless. "Once, I turned the skidder over, and it slid backwards down the mountain. I rode it all the way down, and when it came to a stop, I breathed a sigh of relief only to have one of the saws come loose in the cab and hit me in the

Mutt and Christy on their wedding day

head. I broke a collar bone and some ribs. Fingers. My foot. But nothing serious!"

Mutt married his wife, Christy, on November 10, 2014, high atop a mountain peak on a warm autumn day. My husband, Billy, had the privilege of joining them in marriage. Christy operates the Montebello Camping/Fishing Resort owned by her dad, Charles Grant. During the interview, Christy rolled her eyes at Mutt's "non-serious" injuries and said she was thankful that Timmy and Jason are now working with her husband in the woods.

Ray Ramsey at the Piney River Mill

Over the years, Mutt has hauled to various sawmills in the vicinity, but the day we came for photographs, he was hauling to B. T. Ramsey and Son in Piney River, which is run by Ray Ramsey.

When asked what the downside of logging is, Mutt said, "The worst part is when nothing goes right. Some days, things go smooth, and you can get a load out easy with no problems. Other days are a bear from start to end. Like hollow trees that don't fall straight or an eight- to twelve-thousand-dollar equipment breakdown. You may make good money if you're rolling in lucky and don't have too many of those kinds of breakdowns."

On the upside, Mutt said that he never gets bored doing the same type of work, because each day is different. "No tree falls the same, and you're never in the same area. You are outside, and you're your own boss."

As the interview wound down, I asked what part of logging Mutt Humphreys liked best. He smiled and said, "Going to the mill. The work's over, and the money's come!"

Anna Segedi (Lynn's mom) by the TV in the early 1950s

25

"Old-Time TV Programs"

I am not a die-hard, devoted TV person. I was disturbed by what was being shown on national television back in the 1970s when my eight-year-old daughter was getting an inappropriate dose of after-school education from the soap operas at our babysitter's house. Needless to say, when we moved here in 1980, the TV didn't come with us.

But during my growing-up years, TV programming was superb. Half-hour shows had meaning and moral fiber, teaching youngsters lessons in what was right and acceptable. The bad guys wore black hats, and the good guys wore white. It was as simple as that.

Our family had an upright cabinet style RCA, with a hundred knobs of which only the on/off, volume, and channel selection worked. It had gold-threaded netting across the front, and programs were in glorious black and white. In the early 1950s, they came out with a piece of plastic that you could attach to the screen that had three distinct lines of color: red, green, and blue. This was the forerunner of color TV, but, sadly, it was pretty . . . well, sad.

Many was the morning I'd make a tent under the dining room table while my mother would iron and watch the Arthur Godfrey show. I'd peek out from under the crocheted tablecloth long enough to watch Hona Lokie gyrating her hips in time to a Hawaiian hula dance.

Then there were the Ricardos, Desi and Lucy, along with their neighbors, Fred and Ethel Mertz. The show I remember best was when Lucy and Ethel got jobs in a chocolate factory as candy packers. Pieces of chocolate came down a conveyor belt at a certain speed, while the women were instructed to pack them in boxes. The speed was gradually increased in the hopes that the production rate would pick up, but the girls couldn't keep the pace and ended up stuffing the chocolates in their apron pockets and mouths. It was enough to make Lucy's Cuban bandleader husband swear in his native tongue.

There were other great programs, too. Like George Burns and Gracie Allen or Jack Benny and his hired man, Rochester. And when the large Texaco sign came on the screen, I knew it was time for "Uncle Miltie" (Milton Berle) and his seltzer bottle. My mother never missed the *Perry Como Show,* and I can still see Perry, dressed in a button-up cardigan sweater, crooning away.

Saturday morning kiddie shows were part of my weekend routine until 11:00 a.m., when my mother would announce, "The shows are over; go play outside." Before that, I'd be glued to the tube watching Roy Rogers, Dale Evans, and their sidekick Pat Brady in his jeep, Nellybelle; Bugs Bunny and Porky Pig; crows Heckle and Jeckle; Lassie; and my personal favorite, *Fury,* a story about a horse and Joey, the boy who loved him.

Friday nights were family nights in front of the TV. A whole hour of *The Wonderful World of Disney* came on, and I'd wait all week to watch it. Back then, kids were not allowed everyday snack privileges like today, but on Friday nights, we could choose between a bowl of popcorn and a Coke or a Hire's Root Beer float while we watched Walt spin his magic. At nine, we kids were shuffled off to bed, while my dad tuned in the Friday Night Fights.

Who could forget *Howdy Doody* with Buffalo Bob, Clarabell the clown, Chief Thunderthud, Princess Summerfall Winterspring, and Phineas T. Bluster?

I loved the cowboy shows: *Maverick*, *The Rifleman*, *Sugarfoot*, *Rawhide*, and *Bonanza*. And who could forget Ward Bond yelling, "Head 'em up, move 'em out" on *Wagon Train*?

There were so many greats. Shows like *Father Knows Best*, *Leave It to Beaver*, *Superman*, and *The Flintstones*. *The Ed Sullivan Show* and *Mr. Ed*, the talking horse. When *The Beverly Hillbillies* and *Hee Haw* came onto the scene, my dad said they were the dumbest programs he ever saw and predicted that neither show would last out the year. How wrong he turned out to be. Jed and Ellie Mae, Grandpa Jones and the Culhanes were going strong many years later, making us all laugh with their corny humor.

None of us can look back and fail to smile at all the great shows we were raised on. When people still had morals, made all the right choices, and the heroes wearing white hats were really heroes.

Bob Sales, a World War II hero

26

Bob Sales–
World War II Veteran

In the June 2005 *Backroads* newspaper, I interviewed Bob Sales, who fought in the Battle of Normandy. I remember him telling me to keep the tape recording of his memories because, "Honey, this will be valuable one day. It's history." Although I wrote the story and published it in the paper, I'd like to include it in *Crazy Quilt* because it *is* history, and it was my privilege to talk to Bob and hear in his own words the price that was paid by our military men during World War II, securing the freedom of many. September 2, 2019, marks the seventy-fourth anniversary of the end of the war, and Bob was one of the fortunate ones who made it home. This is his story.

The photo of marching soldiers shows part of Company B, 116th Infantry leaving Lynchburg, Virginia, on February 20, 1941, bound for service in World War II. The arrow about midway at the bottom of the picture points to Bob Sales of Madison Heights proudly marching with his regiment as they leave their hometown.

In military talk, D-Day is a term used to denote the day on which a combat attack or operation is to be initiated.

The men of Company B, 116th Infantry leaving Lynchburg, Virginia, February 20, 1941

The most well-known D-Day was on June 6, 1944, the day on which the Battle of Normandy began, commencing the British, United States, and Canadian liberation efforts of mainland Europe from Nazi occupation.

Bob was fifteen-and-a-half years old when he went to enlist in the National Guard. Lying about his age, he was given an application, which he took home and showed his parents, telling them of his intention to join the military. Bob's mother began to fret, but he remembers his father, Robert Sr., saying, "Don't worry, Cora, he won't last a week." Young Bob not only made it through basic training, but he went on to fight in one of the bloodiest battles in history.

Bob joined the National Guard on December 20, 1940, and was inducted into federal service on February 3, 1941. On February 20, 109 enlisted men and five officers, one of whom was Bob's best friend Dick Wright, left the armory at Lynchburg, Virginia, bound for basic training at Fort Meade, Maryland. Bob remembers the weather being very cold and the ground hard as he learned how to be a soldier.

The 2nd platoon of B Company at Ft. Meade, MD

That spring, the men were sent to Camp A. P. Hill in Richmond and then on to North and South Carolina on maneuvers. On their way back from North Carolina on December 7, 1941, the troops stopped at a store, and someone came out to the truck to tell them that Pearl Harbor had been bombed. Bob said that at the time, he didn't even know where Pearl Harbor was located but was soon to find out. "This war was ready to be fought."

His unit was sent to the eastern shore of Maryland, North Carolina, and Florida on larger maneuvers during that summer. One night in October 1942, members of Company B were quietly moved out on trains and sent to New Jersey, where they were kept in confinement. A few nights later, Bob and his platoon were walking up the gangplank of a huge ship on their way to England. They found out later that they were aboard the *Queen Mary*, which had been stripped down and made into a troopship, transporting fifteen thousand soldiers across the sea. Bob said that the huge ship was so fast, it traveled alone instead of in a convoy, so the men had to keep close watch for any enemy submarines in the vicinity.

Once they landed in Scotland, the men were sent to a facility where they were trained by British commandos, the best in the world. From there, they were sent to Salisbury Plain in Wiltshire, England, where Bob remembers marching by a place called Stonehenge, wondering about the significance of the massive vertical stones.

Bob was chosen as one of twenty who would go to Dover, England, to train again with the British commandos, then go on a raid to France. Because of this training, the company commander approached him, saying a radio operator was needed. So Bob was sent to school to learn map reading, as well as how to operate and carry the thirty-five-pound radio the infantry needed.

At that time, the men knew they were close to invading the French coast. One night, Bob's regiment was quietly taken out and told that Company B would be part of the invasion of Normandy. On June 4, 1944, standing on the mother ship and looking at the beach, they saw the machine gun outposts high in the cliffs and wondered how they were going to get out of the landing crafts and onto land without being hit. They were told that the air force was to bomb the beach before the soldiers arrived, providing craters for protection, so they thought they would have cover. The invasion was originally set for June 5, but bad weather set in, so word came from General Eisenhower that the invasion would be early on June 6.

That morning, before they left, Bob went around to each of the buddies he had left Lynchburg with the year before, patted them on the back, and said, "I'll see you on the beach." He said it was an exciting time, and he felt that they were well trained and that most would survive. Company B had six boats, thirty men to a craft. The boats circled the mother ship until all the craft were loaded before hitting the Normandy coast at 7:00 a.m.

The air force planes that were supposed to provide cover for the soldiers had mistakenly flown too far inland, leaving the long stretch of Omaha Beach unprotected. Because of this, the German gunners had a clear shot at their advancing enemies, but there was so much noise from the ships firing and planes flying overhead that this fact was not immediately evident.

Bob recalls that among the thirty men in his boat was his sergeant, Dick Wright. When all the boats were abreast, and they were heading for shore, A Company was supposed to be the first to land, two minutes ahead of B Company. Bob was laden with gear, including the thirty-five-pound radio he had strapped to his back, when the captain told him to jump up and see what he could see.

Bob at left with friend and sergeant, Dick Wright

"At once, I knew something was wrong. All I could see was smoke, fire, and the bodies of soldiers lying motionless in the water and on the shore. The British coxswain of our boat said he couldn't take us in any farther, and he lowered the landing ramp, which exposed us to the Germans. Our captain was the first one off, and immediately the machine guns cut him to pieces. Bullets were flying around us like bees. Dick Wright was the second man off, and I lost sight of him as a huge wave came up and knocked me off the boat, sending me straight to the bottom of the sea because of all the weight I was carrying.

"Underwater, I struggled to get out of the radio that was strapped on me, holding me down. In the process, I lost my gun and food rations for the next several days. When I finally came up, my captain was eight foot in front of me yelling, 'I'm hit, I'm hit.' I started toward him, but when I got there, he had already gone down. I knew there was nothing to do but to try and save my own life. Everywhere I looked, I saw my buddies dead or wounded. I searched frantically for Dick as I slowly swam toward the beach. I was in water up to my neck, and even at that time of year, the temperature was very cold.

"A mortar shell blew up next to me, and although it didn't wound me seriously, the concussion of it left me dazed and groggy. A man I didn't know came by to help strip off my heavy assault jacket, and then he disappeared. I hung onto a log and pushed along toward the beach. All around me, men were screaming and being hit. It was total chaos, and I thought the invasion had failed.

"It took me an hour and a half to reach shore, and the first person I saw was Dick, lying in the sand about ten feet from me. He told me he was hurt, so I started crawling over to him. He rose up on his elbow, trying to get my attention, when a sniper's bullet hit him in the head, killing him instantly. I knew the sniper had seen me, too, so I laid face down in the sand, waiting for the shot that would end my life. I repeated the 23rd Psalm for about thirty minutes, and in that time, I looked back to see what help might be coming, and in a boat, I saw Captain Robert Ware, the battalion doctor from my hometown.

Bob Sales in uniform

"As a medic, he wasn't supposed to come in this soon, and before my eyes, he was hit by machine gun fire and died in the water. I remember thinking if they killed him, they'd kill us all. The next hour is one I have never forgotten as I crawled past dead soldiers, using their bodies for protection. Shells were hitting all around as I slowly tried to crawl to a wall up ahead. Once there, I saw Mac Smith, a buddy of mine who was wounded in the face. I bandaged his eye the best I could as five or six other men showed up, and we started pulling the wounded out of the surf.

"Later, I found out I was the only man who made it out of my boat alive. Other boats came in and finally knocked out the Germans and saved the beachhead at Omaha. I was taken back to a hospital ship, where I was given some pain pills and slept the night."

In a few days, Bob was able to leave the hospital and return to the beach in search of what was left of B Company. When he found them, they thought he had died with all the others. He said the worst part of the invasion was seeing all his buddies killed and having to leave them on the beach.

A few weeks after the invasion, Bob Sales was promoted to sergeant, taking Dick Wright's place. He later became a platoon sergeant with forty-five men under him. On one mission to take a German town, his unit was pinned down in a large field, and Bob crawled back through a ditch to get a tank needed to take out enemy guns. He maneuvered the tank close enough to fire, and although he did wipe out the German gunners, a rocket hit the tank and shrapnel blew Bob onto the ground, blinding him in both eyes. Later that day, the American soldiers attacked and took the town. Bob was sent back to England for treatment, but they lacked the facilities, so he was sent stateside to a hospital in Valley Forge, Pennsylvania, that specialized in eye surgery. He spent the next year and a half there, having one operation after another to save his right eye. His left eye was permanently blinded. Bob was still in the hospital when the war finally ended in 1945.

In March 1946, Bob was discharged from the army and came home. He was three months short of celebrating his twenty-first birthday. He went into the timber and pulpwood business with an older man, with the stipulation that he'd buy out the man in five years. Bob operated the Sales and White Timber Company for the next forty years, buying land in Nelson and Amherst counties of Virginia. He retired in 1982 but continued to buy and sell land until he became disabled.

Bob Sales was decorated for his military service and received a Purple Heart with two oak-leaf clusters, a Presidential Citation

Bob at grave of Capt. Robert Ware

American graves, Omaha Beach, Normandy, France

with an oak-leaf cluster, a Combat Infantry Badge, and three Battle Stars, including the Silver Star and Bronze Star. On February 12, 2014, Bob and his family traveled to Arlington, where he was presented with the French Legion of Honor by the French president, Francois Hollande. He returned to England and to France, where he visited the graves where his friends who were killed in the battle are buried. He built a private memorial at his home to honor the 113 men who were killed in B Company during World War II and had many Army Buddy Reunions at this site.

Of the original 109 men who left Lynchburg back in 1941, only two were still living in 2005: Bob Sales and Odell Padgett, both of Madison Heights.

As the interview came to a close, Bob ended with this profound statement: "This year, when you hang out your flag, remember that the price of our freedom was paid for with the lives of many."

Bob Sales and his wife Alice in 2005

Robert Luther "Bob" Sales Sr. (89) of Madison Heights passed away on Monday, February 23, 2015, at the Virginia Baptist Hospital in Lynchburg, Virginia.

Sadie Kinsinger and William Hershberger team up at the schnitzing

27

Apple Schnitzing

The term *schnitz* originated from the Pennsylvania Dutch word *snitz*, which refers to a dried chunk of apple, and the German word *schnitzen*, meaning to carve or slice. Cutting up bushels of apples for drying or making apple butter is time-consuming, repetitive work, so gathering many people together to do the job makes for an enjoyable evening of fun, or, as the old adage goes, "Many hands make light work."

Apples take on a much different flavor and texture when they are dried. Through dehydration, moisture is removed, which concentrates the flavor. Packing them in airtight containers will keep the apples edible for up to a year, longer if frozen. Dried apples are a healthful snack and can be soaked in water or cider to rehydrate and then used in cooking and baking, much like fresh apples.

This annual tradition by members of the Amish/Mennonite community of Stuarts Draft has been going on for over fifty years and is sponsored by Pilgrim Fellowship Mennonite Church. In earlier years, the cutting and drying of apples was held at the old cannery located in Draft. It is now held at the former Mt. Zion Amish School during the fall harvest season. The 2018 schnitzing was held every other

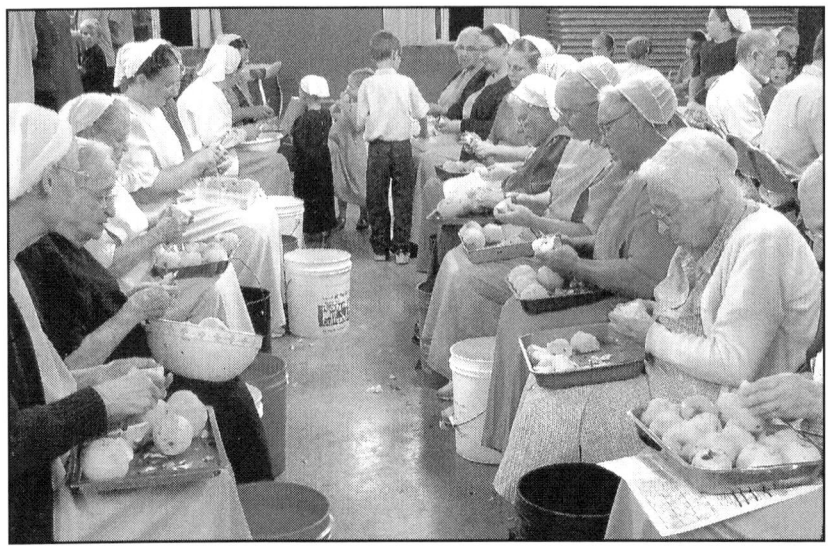

"Many hands make light work"

Apples dropping into crates and taken inside for slicing

Tuesday evening from September 25 through November 20, except one Tuesday night in October when the church holds its yearly revival. The schnitzing was open to the public, as well as the Amish community.

My husband and I were invited to the schnitzing by Mrs. Sadie Kinsinger, and the evening we attended, around fifty-five people were in the process of peeling, coring, and slicing thirty-five bushels of apples. From children to teens to adults, everyone participated.

Paul Hershberger showing the peeling process

Young people working and socializing

Twins Olivia and Veronica Hershberger pitch in

Smaller children carried peeled apples to the adults for cutting and picked up the core leavings. Older children, strong enough to lift a five-gallon bucket of cut apples, carried them to the dryer and poured them in. Happy chatter and laughter permeated the school as people worked side by side throughout the evening.

It was thought that Jonas Kanagy was responsible for manufacturing the large dryer used for the schnitzing activities. The dryer, a propane furnace with forced air circulating under a large metal grid, can dry up to thirty-five bushels of apples at one time. It takes approximately thirty hours to completely dry that amount. When dry, the apples are packed in liners fitted inside fifty-five- gallon drums and sealed.

The idea of sending dried apples to impoverished countries came when Clyde Bender, Jonas Kanagy, and Hershel Bridge went on a mission trip to Haiti and saw the poor living conditions and hunger that existed there. They came back and shared their concerns with their churches and began making plans to send dried apples to a children's home based in Leogane, Haiti. They've done this through the Blue Ridge Mission in Plain City, Ohio, which is a collection site; the mission, in turn, ships the apples, as well as many other products, to Haiti.

Every Tuesday of the schnitzing, Paul and Barbara Hershberger drive their truck to Fitzgerald Orchard in Tyro to pick up forty bushels of apples for that night's cutting. Thirty-five bushels are cut up, and the remaining five bushels are sold to anyone wanting to purchase fresh apples. As a rule of thumb, Paul said they usually try for seven to eight cuttings a year and deliver around twelve drums to the mission in Ohio before they are shipped to Haiti.

Travis Miller carrying apples to the dryer

Jonas Kanagy's propane-fueled dryer

Willis Miller intent on his work

The Leogane Children's Home is a home for girls whose families live in the mountainous regions of Haiti, one of the poorest economic areas of the country. In addition to their regular schoolwork, the girls are taught trades such as crocheting, basketry, and making Caribbean vanilla. Bringing it closer to home, Elizabeth Showalter, daughter of Trent and Marie Showalter, volunteers at the facility. On return trips home, she brings back the girls' handiwork and takes it to the Cheese Shop of Stuarts Draft, where it is sold without commission. Profits go back to support the less fortunate in Haiti.

Another project has been spearheaded by the Trent Showalter family, who collect bars of used soap from hotels and motels in the Waynesboro, Staunton, and Lexington areas. After collection, the soap is cleaned, packaged, and sent to the Leogane Children's Home where it is melted down, formed into balls, and distributed to Haiti's mountain people for personal use and for washing clothes.

As with many other acts of kindness and love, the members of the Amish/Mennonite community pay for their charitable gifts to the less fortunate out of their own pockets, with no cost to the recipient. They are called the "Plain People,"

Leogane Children's Home girls receiving dried apples
(Courtesy of Elizabeth Showalter)

but their message is profound. At Christmas and throughout the year, may we follow their example and find ways to give back to mankind in the name of God's love.

Note: Special thanks to Sadie Kinsinger;
Paul and Barbara Hershberger;
Willis Miller; and Trent, Marie, and Elizabeth Showalter
for kindly providing the information for this article.

Milford Hartman on his zero-turn mower

28

Milford Hartman–
A Centenarian Recalls One Hundred Years of Living

Over the many years of interviewing people for the Backroads books, it has been a real privilege to have talked to quite a few women over the age of one hundred. While giving a talk about the mountain people, someone asked why I had never interviewed a man who had reached the century mark. An older gentleman stood up and addressed the crowd of mostly women and said, "That's because you worry us all to death!"

I'm happy to say that Milford Hartman has defied the odds and reached his one hundredth milestone on December 21, 2018. I didn't find out about Milford until this book was almost completed, but I wanted to include his story because, well . . . simply put, he's an amazing man. He knows a lot of people, and most of them he calls friends. Although Milford enjoys talking about the past, he is up to date on current events as well. He is content to stay in the background because, in his words, "I'm not an up-front kind of person." For that reason, I am delighted he agreed to talk to me about his one hundred years of living. This one is for the men!

Peter S. Hartman (70), Jacob D. (46), Walter E. (24), Walter's son, Floid (2), January 13, 1917

Milford Hartman is still living in his own home and doing quite well. He gets around without the use of a walker or cane and hardly ever goes to the doctor. He drives to church, the post office, and grocery store in Stuarts Draft and treks over to Waynesboro and Staunton whenever he feels like it. His memory is intact, and his conversation is peppered with good humor. The day of the interview, I enjoyed talking with him and his daughter, Barbara, as he reminisced about his life and family.

The baby cradle Milford's great-grandfather, Peter, gave to the family

Milford's great-grandfather, Peter S. Hartman, gave the family a handmade baby cradle that future children slept in. His paternal grandparents were Jacob and Eurie Hartman, Mennonites from the Harrisonburg, Virginia, area. The Hartmans had three sons: Walter, Dan, and Carl. Milford's father was Wilber Carl Hartman (April 8, 1897–June 8, 1933), who married Elizabeth Showalter (June 22, 1894–April 30, 1979). Elizabeth's family lived on a large farm just outside of Lyndhurst, and they, too, were of the Mennonite faith. Elizabeth's father, Samuel James Showalter (July 25, 1853–1919), and his wife, Sarah Good (November 22, 1863–January 8, 1938), bought the farm that bordered the South River from Henry B. and Anna Weaver in 1893.

In later years, the Showalters gave several of their grown children seventy-acre farms in the area. The house and land Elizabeth received was where she and Carl lived when they got married. (It is now owned by the Waynesboro Nursery.) After her father died, they sold that farm to the Quillen

Eurie and Jacob Hartman with their sons, Walter, Dan, and Carl

family and bought out her sibling's part of the original homeplace, and the Hartmans went back to take care of Elizabeth's mother.

Milford's parents married on December 27, 1917. During World War I, Carl was drafted and was due to be sent for active duty, but the war ended, and the military turned him loose just three days before his firstborn son, Milford DeWitt, came into the world on December 21, 1918. Mil-

Samuel James Showalter, before his marriage in the 1880s

Samuel James Showalter II with his mother, Sarah Good Showalter

ford's sisters, Sara Frances and Phyllis, came next. His only brother, Robert, was the fourth child born to the Hartmans, and baby Mildred completed the family. Of the five siblings, only Milford and his sister Mildred, now eighty-eight years of age, survive.

Milford's father kept milk cows and

Showalter siblings: (Top L–R) Samuel II, Mary, Willie; (Bottom L–R) Ada, John, Mattie, and Elizabeth

The Showalter homeplace

began operating the "Early Dawn (Carl Hartman) Dairy" at the homeplace located between US 340 and Lyndhurst Road. He remembers they delivered milk to a small country store near the entrance of the CCC Camp at Sand Spring, as well as their Waynesboro route.

In 1925, Carl's brother Walter became a partner, and the company changed its name to "Early Dawn (Hartman Brother's) Dairy." A separate home was built for Walter, who moved to the farm from Illinois. Walter later left the company, and over the years, a series of different people rented the house where he had lived. In 1943, Milford's brother Robert married Hilda Massie, and in 1944, they moved into Walter's old home and remained there until both of their deaths. The couple's only child, Brenda, who grew up in the home and later moved in to take care of her parents, continues to live there.

Carl and Elizabeth Showalter Hartman

Although Carl must have started out delivering milk with a horse and wagon, Milford's first memory of the dairy was when his dad had one truck. Then he remembers two and later, a third. They delivered to the Waynesboro residents first and next to the various stores, such as Colonial, A&P, and Paddy's Grocery on Main Street, which was an independent store owned by A. P. Paddy. They also delivered milk to two hotels, the Fairfax and the Brunswick.

Four of the five Hartman children: Phyllis, Robert, Sara Frances, and Milford

Early Dawn Dairy in operation

In 1926, D. H. Wright joined the dairy operation. At that time, there were a number of area farmers who had cows and sold their excess milk to surrounding neighbors. Some of these were Julian Pratt; Frank Clark; Joe Driver; Milford's uncle, O. C. Flory; and Abner Weaver. Weaver made deliveries in a Ford panel truck with "Shenandoah Dairy" painted on the side.

A Hartman Farm milk bottle

In 1929, Abner Weaver merged into the Early Dawn group, and in 1932, O. C. Flory, who owned Village End Dairy in Stuarts Draft, joined to form a co-op. This co-op was incorporated as Early Dawn Co-Operative Dairy, and the whole operation was moved to Waynesboro, where a portion of the Crystal Fount ice plant could be utilized for refrigeration. Other milk producers who later joined the co-op were A. E. Houff, J. R.

The house built for Walter Hartman

Driver, T. O. Tench, Fay K. Koiner, Mrs. Carl Hartman, J. A. Wilson, Amos Showalter, and Clay Hewitt, who supplied cream to the Early Dawn Dairy.

One of the Early Dawn Dairy trucks

The Hartmans made hay for their animals and had a large vegetable garden for fresh food; they canned the excess for the winter months. Milford said, "Back in the 1920s and '30s, if you didn't have a garden, you'd starve to death."

The Hartman farm

Everyone in the family worked, and Milford laughed as he said, "There was no loafing back then. In the 1930s, there were men who rode the trains . . . hoboes who came to the house and would do a bit of work for a meal. My dad would send them out to the woodpile and tell them they could split wood and get their lunch."

The Hartmans kept a herd of Guernsey, Jersey, and Holstein cows. They milked twice a day by hand until a milking machine was bought, making the operation easier and more efficient. They had a large bank barn with an upper floor where hay was stored, a basement where the cows were milked and fed, and a stable on the opposite end where their Clydesdale workhorses were kept. Milford remembers that his grandmother had a beautiful black horse named Maude that pulled a buggy, and he would take her around to visit some of the neighbors, like the Arnolds.

Milford recalls, "Once, I was riding the mare out in the pasture fields to get the cows and had to cross a plowed field. I was galloping back, and she tramped in a furrow and fell, breaking her neck. Another time, I was riding a pony down by the river, and the pony throwed me off. It didn't hurt me, and I walked home, but that night when I got ready for bed and took off my shirt, there was a hoofprint right in the middle of my back!"

He learned to swim in the South River by tying a rope to the bushes and trees on either side of the river and hanging on to it, kicking his feet and paddling along.

In the elementary grades, Milford attended Hall School, which was located next to Springdale Mennonite Church; later, he graduated from Stuarts Draft High School.

Milford said that his first car was a 1934 Ford convertible, and when I smiled and rolled my eyes, he laughed and said, "Yes, I was a big dog back then!" He recalled that there was a low place on Barterbrook Road where the water came across, and they would pull their cars in the water to wash them. He also had a 1924 Model T truck. He knocked the muffler loose with a

Ellen Showalter at eighteen years old

pipe wrench so you could hear it coming a mile away. "It sounded so *good!*"

Milford first saw his future wife at Greenville High School during a basketball game where he was playing for Stuarts Draft High. He thought to himself, "Boy, that's a beautiful lady. I sure would like to meet her." About a year later, he got the chance when the Greenville High School closed and became part of Stuarts Draft High School, and he formally met Ellen Myrtle Coyner. They dated for several years before marrying on December 27, 1938.

The couple lived in a little house close to the river on the Showalter farm. Their daughter, Barbara, was born there on July 13, 1940, and son, Roger, on October 27, 1942. While living in that particular house, the oil heater malfunctioned one night, and oily black soot blew everywhere. All they could see of Barbara was the whites of her eyeballs.

Ellen, Milford, and Barbara Jean

Through the years, the Showalter and Hartman families attended Springdale Mennonite Church, but just before

Milford and Ellen married, they began going to Stuarts Draft Baptist Church, where they were wed in the parsonage. Back then, the church was located on Main Street in Draft, but later, a new brick church was built on Route 340, and that is where Milford continues to attend.

Milford is a World War II veteran, drafted into the military in 1944 at twenty-seven years of age. He became a ground crewman for an aircraft unit at a naval air station. He started out at the US Naval Airbase in Seattle, Washington, home of the Naval Air Transport Service (NATS) at Sand Point, and was shipped to Alaska and later to the Aleutian Islands. He was with a group who flew cargo planes that also transported people, and his job as a ground crewman was to make sure the planes were filled with gas and to check the oil and the de-icer tanks.

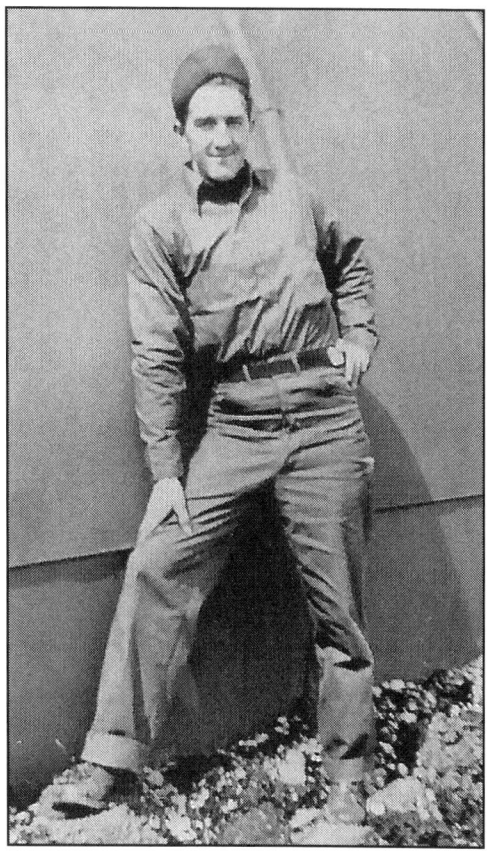

Milford 1945-46 in the Aleutian Islands

He served two years, coming home for good in January 1946. He is proud of his service to his country and is equally proud of his son, Roger, and grandson Bryan Gray, who followed in his footsteps and served in the military. While he was in the navy, Ellen and the children stayed with her parents until his return.

Milford with Barbara Jean and Roger

When the children were growing up, the Hartmans lived in and around the Waynesboro, Stuarts Draft, and Greenville areas, with one move to Emporia where Milford worked at a textile plant. Closer to home, he found employment at the Celanese Plant in Verona, Wayne Manufacturing, and the General Electric Plant in Waynesboro, from which he retired in November 1981. Earlier in her life, Ellen was a stay-at-home mother who had time to raise her children and take care of the home. She later worked eleven years and retired from the General Electric Plant.

In the 1950s, when Barbara was in high school, her parents bought an acre of land in Stuarts Draft and had a brick

Ellen and Milford in later years

rancher built on top of a little knoll overlooking the mountains. It's a warm and cozy house, with family photos sitting here and there, along with all kinds of mementos from Milford's long life.

The extended Hartman family today

He and Ellen were married for seventy-four happy years before she passed away on February 2, 2014, and Milford said he misses her to this day. In addition to their two children, the Hartmans have five grandchildren, seven great-grandchildren, and a great-great-grandson, Jackson.

As the interview wound down, Milford imparted a few words of wisdom that most would have to agree with. "I think we've already seen this country's best years; from the 1950s after the war, on up through the 1980s. We've enjoyed more peace and less trouble than any time in history."

I asked Milford what his secret is to living such a long and fruitful life, and he was quick to reply, "I've always tried to live by the Golden Rule."

Milford Hartman relaxing at his home

The author at the Dodd Cabin, Beech Grove

About the Author

Even as a child, Lynn had a Waldenish bent toward a nineteenth-century existence, despite the fact that she was being raised by city parents and growing up along the busy Gold Coast of southern Florida, with all the amenities of modern living. Her dream was to someday build a log cabin in the mountains and live a quiet, self-sufficient lifestyle.

Lynn began living that dream upon moving to the tiny hamlet of Love, Virginia, in the summer of 1980. As she met and got to know her neighbors, all of whom were quite elderly at the time, she soon realized that the culture of these hearty Scottish/Irish descendants was slowly ebbing away and somehow needed to be preserved.

Without any formal education or prior experience in journalism, Lynn carved out a folksy niche, documenting early Appalachian life through the pages of a monthly newspaper that she and her neighbor, Bunny Stein, created called *Backroads*. The first issue was published in December 1981.

Bunny left the after the first year, and Lynn published the newspaper solo for the next twenty-four years. *Backroads* chronicled the early history of the mountain people, and

Lynn traveled the hills and hollers to interview the native elders and photograph them, as well as their handicrafts and the activities that had been handed down for generations.

Little did she realize how entwined her life would become with theirs or how much the mountain people would come to mean to her as they opened their hearts to trust a young woman who had started out as a Florida flatlander and ended up becoming one of them.

When she stopped publishing *Backroads* in December 2006, the mountain people's cry, "Don't let our stories die with your retirement," haunted Lynn. She began compiling the articles from the old newspaper and put them into book form. Five books about the Appalachian culture resulted: *Plain Folk and Simple Livin'*, *The Road to Chicken Holler*, *Faces of Appalachia*, *Appalachian Heart*, and *Mountain Folk*. *Crazy Quilt* is the sixth book of the series.

Lynn believes that God has his hand on each individual and has a certain task he wants each to accomplish during the years he gives them on earth. Lynn's advice to the world at large is, "Find your path, and do not stray from it. Walk resolutely toward your goal and don't let anyone discourage you from your dreams. Because . . .

> *If you do what God has called you to do, in the end, you will be fulfilled, and the world will be blessed."*

You can order additional copies of *Crazy Quilt* or other books by Lynn Coffey by using this order form.

ORDER FORM

Name _____

Address _____

City, State, Zip _____

Crazy Quilt	_____ copies
Mountain Folk	_____ copies
Appalachian Heart	_____ copies
Backroads	_____ copies
Backroads 2	_____ copies
Backroads 3	_____ copies

The price of each book is $20.00. Please add $3.50 for shipping for each copy ordered. Make checks or money orders payable to Lynn Coffey and mail to:

Lynn Coffey
1461 Love Road
Lyndhurst, VA 22952

Made in the USA
Middletown, DE
22 May 2019